SANCTIONS AND FINANCIAL PRESSURE: MAJOR NATIONAL SECURITY TOOLS

HEARING

BEFORE THE

COMMITTEE ON FOREIGN AFFAIRS
HOUSE OF REPRESENTATIVES

ONE HUNDRED FIFTEENTH CONGRESS

SECOND SESSION

JANUARY 10, 2018

Serial No. 115–107

Printed for the use of the Committee on Foreign Affairs

Available via the World Wide Web: http://www.foreignaffairs.house.gov/ or
http://www.gpo.gov/fdsys/

U.S. GOVERNMENT PUBLISHING OFFICE

28–178PDF   WASHINGTON : 2018

COMMITTEE ON FOREIGN AFFAIRS

EDWARD R. ROYCE, California, *Chairman*

CHRISTOPHER H. SMITH, New Jersey
ILEANA ROS-LEHTINEN, Florida
DANA ROHRABACHER, California
STEVE CHABOT, Ohio
JOE WILSON, South Carolina
MICHAEL T. McCAUL, Texas
TED POE, Texas
DARRELL E. ISSA, California
TOM MARINO, Pennsylvania
MO BROOKS, Alabama
PAUL COOK, California
SCOTT PERRY, Pennsylvania
RON DeSANTIS, Florida
MARK MEADOWS, North Carolina
TED S. YOHO, Florida
ADAM KINZINGER, Illinois
LEE M. ZELDIN, New York
DANIEL M. DONOVAN, JR., New York
F. JAMES SENSENBRENNER, JR.,
  Wisconsin
ANN WAGNER, Missouri
BRIAN J. MAST, Florida
FRANCIS ROONEY, Florida
BRIAN K. FITZPATRICK, Pennsylvania
THOMAS A. GARRETT, JR., Virginia
JOHN R. CURTIS, Utah

ELIOT L. ENGEL, New York
BRAD SHERMAN, California
GREGORY W. MEEKS, New York
ALBIO SIRES, New Jersey
GERALD E. CONNOLLY, Virginia
THEODORE E. DEUTCH, Florida
KAREN BASS, California
WILLIAM R. KEATING, Massachusetts
DAVID N. CICILLINE, Rhode Island
AMI BERA, California
LOIS FRANKEL, Florida
TULSI GABBARD, Hawaii
JOAQUIN CASTRO, Texas
ROBIN L. KELLY, Illinois
BRENDAN F. BOYLE, Pennsylvania
DINA TITUS, Nevada
NORMA J. TORRES, California
BRADLEY SCOTT SCHNEIDER, Illinois
THOMAS R. SUOZZI, New York
ADRIANO ESPAILLAT, New York
TED LIEU, California

AMY PORTER, *Chief of Staff*   THOMAS SHEEHY, *Staff Director*
JASON STEINBAUM, *Democratic Staff Director*

CONTENTS

Page

WITNESSES

The Honorable Juan C. Zarate, chairman and co-founder, Financial Integrity Network (former Assistant Secretary for Terrorist Financing and Financial Crimes, U.S. Department of the Treasury) 3
Mr. Derek Maltz, executive director, Governmental Relations, Pen-Link, Ltd. (former Special Agent in Charge, Special Operations Division, Drug Enforcement Administration, U.S. Department of Justice) 26
Mr. Adam Szubin, distinguished practitioner-in-residence, Johns Hopkins University School of Advanced International Studies (former Acting Under Secretary for Terrorism and Financial Intelligence, U.S. Department of the Treasury) 37

LETTERS, STATEMENTS, ETC., SUBMITTED FOR THE HEARING

The Honorable Juan C. Zarate: Prepared statement 6
Mr. Derek Maltz: Prepared statement 29
Mr. Adam Szubin: Prepared statement 40

APPENDIX

Hearing notice 84
Hearing minutes 85
The Honorable Steve Chabot, a Representative in Congress from the State of Ohio, and chairman, Subcommittee on Asia and the Pacific: Material submitted for the record 87
The Honorable Gerald E. Connolly, a Representative in Congress from the Commonwealth of Virginia: Prepared statement 90
The Honorable William Keating, a Representative in Congress from the Commonwealth of Massachusetts: Questions submitted for the record 92

SANCTIONS AND FINANCIAL PRESSURE: MAJOR NATIONAL SECURITY TOOLS

WEDNESDAY, JANUARY 10, 2018

House of Representatives,
Committee on Foreign Affairs,
Washington, DC.

The committee met, pursuant to notice, at 10:09 a.m., in room 2172, Rayburn House Office Building, Hon. Ed Royce (chairman of the committee) presiding.

Chairman ROYCE. We will call the committee to order.

Today the hearing is on "Sanctions and Financial Pressure: Major National Security Tools." And I will begin by saying that this committee has played a leading role in applying sanctions and related elements of financial pressure to address major U.S. national security threats. We have used America's economic might to help stop terrorists, to counter Iran and North Korea's nuclear programs, and to respond to Russian aggression and the degradation of democracy in Venezuela.

Today we are joined by three former officials with unique experience in using these economic tools, and their testimony will help us ensure that the sanctions we have enacted are fully imple- mented while improving our ability to draft tough, effective legisla- tion going forward.

Last summer, in response to the ongoing threats from Iran, Russia, and North Korea, it was this committee that put together legislation, it was Congress that enacted the Countering America's Adversaries Through Sanctions Act to affect all three. The administration faces a deadline to implement key elements of this act by the end of the month. It is this committee's expectation that this deadline be met.

Meanwhile, later this week the President faces a decision on the Iran nuclear agreement. Senior members of this committee were united in bipartisan opposition to the Obama administration's deeply flawed deal which handed over roughly $100 billion in sanctions relief in return for temporary restrictions on Iran's nuclear program. This sunset flaw and other serious problems need to be fixed. We must make certain that international inspectors have access to possible nuclear sites, particularly those on military bases.

And at the same time we have got to continue to counter the full range of threats posed by the corrupt and dangerous regime in Teheran that is—at this moment—brutally cracking down on the people of Iran. And that is where the committee has already taken the lead, because yesterday on the House, and many of the members here spoke on that issue, we passed a resolution, 415 to 2, which we drafted, calling for additional sanctions on those responsible for human rights abuses.

Additionally, we have passed legislation through the House targeting Iran's ballistic missile program, and we are working with our colleagues in the Senate to strengthen the Hezbollah International Financing Prevention Act. This is a landmark bill enacted 2 years ago to target Iran's top terror proxy, Hezbollah. The Obama administration let up on Hezbollah in order to get the Iran nuclear deal, and one of our witnesses will note how this legislation can keep that from happening again.

And yesterday, two of our members, Chairman Mike McCaul, Representative Ted Deutch, they introduced a bill to target Iranian officials involved in human rights abuses and hostage taking. The committee is also working on a bill designed to help push the Revolutionary Guards out of Iran's economy and deny them the revenue that they use to destabilize Iraq and destabilize Syria and Lebanon, all while continuing to threaten Israel. And this is the abuse and corruption and the expensive interference in neighboring countries that brave Iranians have taken to the streets to protest.

So our efforts against the Revolutionary Guards and Hezbollah are prime examples of how what we often call "sanctions" are really a broader set of tools, from disclosure and due-diligence requirements to civil and criminal investigations.

When it comes to the threat from North Korea, I have called for the "primary money laundering concern" designation against large Chinese banks that continue to do business with the Kim Jong-un regime. As another of our witnesses knows, this major tool was used with great effect when the Treasury Department targeted Banco Delta Asia in 2006. We must stop Kim Jong-un from building a reliable nuclear arsenal capable of striking the United States.

Sanctions are rooted in Article I power to regulate commerce with foreign nations. So it is not surprising that Congress has had to push successive administrations to effectively use these national security tools. No matter how tough the language of our sanctions bills, they are only as strong as their enforcement. And that is why we must work together to ensure that the executive branch not only has the political will, but also the growing resources, as well as the expertise needed, to implement stronger sanctions. So we look forward to hearing from our witnesses on how to do exactly that.

We are going to come back later for the opening statement from our ranking member, who is on his way. But let me go now to the introduction of our witnesses, our distinguished panel here.

Mr. Juan Zarate is the chairman and co-founder of the Financial Integrity Network, and previously, as the members of this committee well know, Mr. Zarate was the Assistant Secretary of the Treasury for Terrorist Financing and Financial Crimes.

Mr. Derek Maltz is the executive director of government relations at Pen-Link. Previously, Mr. Maltz led the Drug Enforcement Administration's Special Operations Division in actively targeting narcotics trafficking tied to Hezbollah.

And both of these gentlemen were involved in other operations that involve those of us on the committee as well. We appreciate their service, as we do Mr. Adam Szubin, because he also has assisted this country mightily in these endeavors. He is a distinguished practitioner-in-residence at Johns Hopkins School of Advanced International Studies. And previously he was the Acting Undersecretary of the Treasury for Terrorism and Financial Intelligence.

Without objection, the witnesses' full prepared statements will be made part of the record. Members here will have 5 calendar days to submit any questions that you might have or extraneous materials for the record.

So if you would, Mr. Zarate, please open, and feel free to summarize your remarks. And after your 5 minutes and each of the panel members speak, we will go to questions.

STATEMENT OF THE HONORABLE JUAN C. ZARATE, CHAIRMAN AND CO-FOUNDER, FINANCIAL INTEGRITY NETWORK (FORMER ASSISTANT SECRETARY FOR TERRORIST FINANCING AND FINANCIAL CRIMES, U.S. DEPARTMENT OF THE TREASURY)

Mr. ZARATE. Well, Mr. Chairman, thank you for the invitation to be here today before you and this committee. I want to thank you and the distinguished members of this committee for holding the hearing and for your time and attention.

Before I start, Mr. Chairman, I want to thank you for your years of service. As a proud native son of Orange County, California, I am proud of your service, grateful for it, and know that I have had the privilege of working with you on these very issues that we will be discussing today.

And, in fact, Mr. Maltz and I had the privilege of working on the issue of Viktor Bout, of which you played a major part in making sure that he was eventually captured and put in jail here the United States.

I want to thank you for your years of service to this country.

[Applause.]

Chairman ROYCE. I thank you, Mr. Zarate. I appreciate that very much.

I do notice a constituent of mine over your shoulder. Would you care to introduce your sister?

Mr. ZARATE. I would love to, Mr. Chairman. I am not used to having family members with me, but I am really honored and pleased to have my sister with me, Marisa Zarate Zweiback. She is moving from Pasadena, California, actually.

She just retired after nearly three decades of service as a Los Angeles County deputy district attorney. And she has devoted her life to public safety and security, and I am privileged to have her as my sister.

Chairman ROYCE. We would like to welcome her here as well. Thank you.

Mr. ZARATE. Mr. Chairman, this is an important moment, as you know, to take stock of the critical role that financial measures, including sanctions—not just sanctions, as you indicated—play in our national security. These measures have become the tools often of first resort and even our central strategies in dealing with the hardest national security challenges facing our country.

And as we rely and the international community relies more heavily on economic coercion in statecraft, it becomes critical to ensure their effectiveness and that the U.S. can continue to lead and use them effectively on an international basis. Congress, obviously, plays a key role in this endeavor.

This is especially important as the targets of U.S. measures adapt to pressure, and they do. The financial and economic environment globally grows more interdependent and complicated, and they leverage that. Competitors and adversaries seek to displace or even undermine U.S. dominance as well as the U.S. dollar in the international financial system. And as we see new technologies come online in the fintech space and with cryptocurrencies, the question of whether or not illicit activity is further enabled globally becomes a challenge.

So this is an important moment to talk about the principles and issues tied to the use of these measures. Let me just indicate some core principles to how I think we should deploy these measures.

In the first instance, strategy matters, Mr. Chairman, as you know. Any attempt to use sanctions or financial measures has to nest and sit within a coherent strategy and cannot stand alone.

Second, the economic toolkit must be seen as a broader set of coercive tools that are more effective when deployed in concert to shape the environment.

Third, for financial pressure to actually work it must be applied and enforced constantly to identify and isolate targeted behavior. It is like weeding a garden. It has to be done consistently to shape the environment.

Fourth, there must be a focus on conduct-based activities that violate international norms and principles. We are beginning to see that more and more in the context of human rights abuses, corruption, and violation of international sanctions.

Fifth, there has to be a recognition and an understanding, I think it is critical for legislation, that a core pillar of not just the system but what makes these measures work is that we are also protecting the integrity of the financial system. That means that financial regulations tie very neatly and are dependent on sanctions and vice versa.

In addition, we have to have creativity and flexibility in our approach and application. It is not a one-size-fits-all approach to sanctions and it is not always a maximalist approach that will get you the best results.

Finally, the United States has to play the leading role still, I believe, in enforcing these measures and in setting the norms internationally. That is what will endure in terms of our ability to use these tools effectively.

Mr. Chairman, there is urgency in action to make sure we do this right given the weight put on these tools and strategies. In the case of North Korea, there must be an all-out campaign to leverage financial information, sanctions, interdictions, related financial measures, to squeeze the regime's finances and access to capital.

More importantly, these measures should be used to attempt to alter the dynamics with China by putting fundamental Chinese interests at risk—without needing to threaten China directly—so they use their leverage to affect Pyongyang's decisionmaking.

With Iran, as you indicated, Mr. Chairman, measures to isolate and pressure the Revolutionary Guard and regime leadership, in part by spotlighting human rights abuses, corruption, support to terrorism and militant proxies, progress on a ballistic missile program which is still subject to U.N. sanctions, all of that can be undertaken right away and with great vigor regardless of one's view on the JCPOA and what should happen next with respect to that deal.

With Russia, the U.S. must retain escalatory dominance, along with European allies, in the use of sanctions and economic statecraft. With sanctions and measures against a major G20 economy, we have to be conscious of the measures that Russia takes in counter and in defense of these measures. And we have to then deal with Russian aggression in Ukraine, Putin's corruption, support for Assad's regime in Syria, related human rights abuses, and, of course, malicious cyber activity.

Finally, Mr. Chairman, with transnational issues like proliferation finance, cyber hacking, kleptocracy, there is an opportunity here to drive financial isolation and the use of these measures to get at the core regimes and actors we want to isolate from the financial system.

The regimes we care most about, the North Koreans, the Iranians, the Russians, are corrupt to the core, and corruption itself is an international norm and standard that we can begin to drive more effectively as a core national security strategy.

Mr. Chairman, I am over my time. I have more to say. I am happy to reserve for questions and answers. But I would just say there is more we can do currently to increase the amount of attention, urgency, and resources to applying these sanctions and measures effectively. Part of that is ensuring the interagency is working together, with full force. Part of that is constant enforcement, as I mentioned. And part of that has to do with being more creative with how we use these tools, both in application and in unwinding.

I think I will leave it there, Mr. Chairman. Thank you, again, for this opportunity.

[The prepared statement of Mr. Zarate follows:]

The Honorable Juan C. Zarate

Chairman and Co-Founder
Financial Integrity Network

Chairman and Senior Counselor
Center on Sanctions and Illicit Finance

Former Deputy Assistant to the President and
Deputy National Security Advisor for Combating Terrorism

Former Assistant Secretary of the Treasury
for Terrorist Financing and Financial Crimes

Testimony before the
U.S. House of Representatives
Foreign Affairs Committee

Sanctions and Financial Pressure:
Major National Security Tools

January 10, 2018

Juan Zarate
Financial Integrity Network

January 10, 2018

Chairman Royce, Ranking Member Engel, and distinguished members of the U.S. House of Representatives Committee on Foreign Affairs, I am honored to be with you today to discuss the role of sanctions and financial pressure in our national security. I want to thank Chairman Royce for his leadership of this Committee and years of diligent work on the Hill and in the foreign policy community. I am grateful for the sober work we did together on issues of national security. Your voice of reason, seriousness of purpose, and compassionate and strong vision for America's place in the world will be missed in Southern California, Congress, and in Washington.

I have been privileged to serve in the U.S. government – at the U.S. Justice Department, the Treasury Department, and at the National Security Council – spending much of my time developing the tools, strategies, and institutions of economic statecraft since September 11th. Among other developments in this period, the establishment of the Office of Terrorism and Financial Intelligence (TFI) at the U.S. Treasury signaled the U.S. government's recognition of the importance of Treasury's tools and suasion, financial intelligence, and financial pressure campaigns in our national security architecture.

Since leaving government in 2009, I have continued to work with think tanks, in academia, and in the consulting worlds to develop the understanding, strategies, and capacity in this space. The publication of my book, "Treasury's War: The Unleashing of a New Era of Financial Warfare," in 2013, was my attempt to explain the evolution and importance of financial and economic tools in our national security – and the critical nature of these issues for the international community in the years to come. Our founding of the Financial Integrity Network (FIN) almost four years ago signaled a desire to help clients meet heightened global expectations of financial integrity, to build the capacity and design new models to address the complexities of this environment, and to make the tools that protect the international financial system more effective. The establishment of the Center on Sanctions and Illicit Finance (CSIF) at the Foundation for Defense of Democracies (FDD) in November 2014, represented our commitment to create a think tank dedicated to developing the doctrines and strategies of national economic security, especially in the face of new challenges to U.S. power.

This background and ongoing work has afforded me insights and learning that I hope will be helpful to this Committee and Congress. Thank you again for the invitation to testify.

This is an important moment to take stock of the critical role that financial measures, including sanctions, play in our national security. These economic and financial tools of coercion have traditionally filled a gap in the national security toolkit between diplomacy and kinetic action. Over the past fifteen years, they have become the tools of first resort and even our central strategies in dealing with the hardest national security challenges facing our country.

Financial pressure campaigns have shaped our approaches to threats from nation states like Iran, North Korea, and Russia and non-state actors like terrorists, human rights violators, and malicious cyber actors; empowered the United States and the international community to address broad sets of transnational threats, like proliferation, transnational organized crime, sanctions evasion, and corruption; and enabled and complemented our diplomacy, law enforcement,

Juan Zarate
Financial Integrity Network

intelligence, and military efforts. These are measures aimed not just at rogue actors but are intended fundamentally to protect the integrity of the U.S. and international financial system.

Importantly, using financial power and suasion to affect America's enemies and their budgets – well beyond U.S. borders – provided a form of asymmetric power that the United States could use against non-state networks exploiting the global system. In many ways, this was a strategic window into a new way to leverage power in the 21st century – which does not require kinetics and relies heavily on the influence and decisions of private sector actors.

These tools can also be seen as convenient to use relative to other national security measures, serving as a clear statement of policy and allowing a public demonstration of the steps taken in response to crises or direct threats. There is a danger of overuse and a diminishment of their value and effectiveness if they are not deployed carefully and with clear strategic intent, especially given the burdens placed on the private sector to implement many of these measures.

As the United States and international community rely more heavily on these tools of economic statecraft, it is critical that we ensure their effectiveness, legitimacy, and preserve and strengthen the ability of the United States to use strategies of economic coercion against threats to U.S. national security. Congress plays a key role in this endeavor.

In recent years, Congress has taken an even more active role in the expansion and use of sanctions and financial measures in U.S. policy, as seen in key pieces of legislation over time like Title III of the USA PATRIOT Act in 2001, the Comprehensive Iran Sanctions, Accountability, and Divestment Act of 2010 (CISADA), the Hizballah International Financing Prevention Act of 2015 (HIFPA), and the Global Magnitsky Human Rights Accountability Act of 2016. This Committee has played a major role in this work. How Congress steers the evolution of the use of financial and economic measures, working together with the Administration, will be critical to the credibility of U.S. efforts and the sustainability of these tools and strategies.

This is especially important as the targets of U.S. measures adapt to pressure, the financial and economic environment globally grows more interdependent and complicated, competitors or adversaries seek to displace or undermine U.S. dominance and the U.S. dollar in the international financial system, and as new technologies enable economic and financial relationships between illicit actors.

Ultimately, the United States has a deep interest in preserving and deepening its ability to protect the integrity of the financial system and marshal economic and financial measures to address national and international security concerns.

Core Principles for the Use of Financial and Economic Measures

There are fundamental principles that should drive any serious use of sanctions, financial measures, or the deployment of an economic pressure campaign. These principles should inform the design, choreography, and strategy deployed before launching any type of sanction or form of economic coercion.

Juan Zarate
Financial Integrity Network

January 10, 2018

1. *Strategy Matters.* To be effective, an attempt to use sanctions or financial measures of any sort must nest within a coherent strategy and cannot stand alone. Too often, sanctions have been seen as either the only retreat for action to address a thorny national security issue, or as a silver bullet that can bend behavior and alter a threat landscape on its own. For any financial pressure campaign to work, it must be in service of an understood strategy and complemented by other tools of statecraft, power, and coercion. These tools can be used to deny access to the global financial and commercial system and disrupt the capabilities of actors in achieving their goals – be it preventing the development of weapons of mass destruction in the case of Iran and North Korea, deterrence against continued aggression as in the case of Russia, or disruption of broad global reach for terrorist groups.

   Ultimately, these are measures that enable the United States and the international community to make it harder, costlier, and riskier for illicit actors and rogue states to raise and move money globally. In maximalist form, these tools can affect the budget, bottom line, and decision-making of the targeted regimes or networks. The strategy of economic coercion must then be crafted to achieve the defined goal.

2. *Coercive Tools in Concert.* The sanctions and economic toolkit must be seen as part of a broader set of coercive tools that are more effective when deployed in concert to shape the environment. In the case of North Korea, interdiction of suspect North Korean shipping, arrests of those involved in North Korean illicit financial activity, broad-based information campaigns to weaken the regime's control of the information environment, and an aggressive focus on the regime's human rights abuses are all complementary and functional parts of any campaign to isolate the North Korean economy and affect the regime's decision-making. These are also tools that should target, impact, and deter those who do business or finance the regime's activities. Sanctions must be seen as part of a broader effort to disrupt the target's ability to resource its ambitions and access the key elements of the financial and commercial system.

3. *Constant, Consistent Pressure and Enforcement.* For a financial pressure campaign to work, it must be applied and enforced constantly to identify and isolate the targeted behavior. Often, U.S. and international sanctions and pressure have suffered from applying an escalatory model based simply on reactions to provocations and violations of existing sanctions. Such sanctions have been perceived as important primarily in aid of diplomacy. Although that is a critical use of these tools, in order to be effective, they must be seen as their own form of pressure, coercion, and disruption that complements our diplomacy. As in the case of North Korea and Russia, some sanctions have been dictated more by the provocations of the regime as opposed to what an effective financial and economic pressure campaign should look like. Any use of sanctions must be part of a broader campaign to sensitize the international community and markets to exclude rogue actors involved with sanctioned parties from the legitimate financial and commercial system. This includes targeting sanctions evasion as its own threat and source of illicit finance worthy of focused enforcement attention. Like weeding a garden, such work has to be consistent and constant, to shape market and governments' behavior.

Juan Zarate
Financial Integrity Network

4. *Conduct-Based Focus.* A successful, sustainable campaign against rogue regimes and dangerous networks that enlists key allies and stakeholders should focus intently on conduct-based sanctions and measures that target the illicit, dangerous, and suspicious activities that violate international norms and principles and put the financial system at risk. A fundamental vulnerability for North Korea is that it is not only developing nuclear weapons capabilities in violation of international sanctions, but it is a criminal state. It is engaged in proliferation, massive human rights abuses, money laundering, corruption, sanctions evasion, counterfeiting, smuggling, drug trafficking, and other nefarious and suspect activities. A clear vulnerability for Iran is that the regime is corrupt, engaged in nefarious and illegal activities (from support to terror to cyber intrusions), and the Islamic Revolutionary Guard Corps controls – overtly and with a hidden hand -- many of the key sectors and elements of the economy.

Illicit or inherently suspect activities are interwoven into how many sanctioned parties do business – and try to avoid sanctions -- and should be isolated by the international community – governments and the private sector alike – regardless of the diplomatic posture. Such activities are the subject of sanctions, criminal laws, and financial regulations. At a time of heightened concern over transparency and accountability in the financial system, there should be no objection to doing so, especially in major economies and legitimate financial centers. As long as sanctions and related efforts to target illicit networks and their supporting financial and commercial infrastructure remain focused on the activities that violate accepted international norms and principles, they will prove more effective and be amplified by the actions of the private sector and actors concerned about real and reputational risk.

5. *Creativity and Flexibility in Application.* The use of sanctions and financial measures must be tailored to the desired strategies and targets, and we must remain open and flexible to new approaches in the application of these tools. The same playbook that has been used successfully for prior campaigns may not be the right approach for the next or a different campaign. A maximalist approach of full financial and economic isolation at once – especially at the outset of a financial and economic pressure campaign -- may not be the most effective way of using these tools. In some cases the mere threat of the use of sanctions, as with secondary sanctions or the potential application of Section 311 of the Patriot Act, can affect behavior and meet desired U.S. goals. In other cases, a phased constriction campaign, addressing specific vulnerabilities, risks, and threats over time, may be most helpful to deter actors or to ensure the longevity and effectiveness of any measures imposed. In addition, there may be a need for more creativity in the use of other kinds of sanctions, regulations, or financial measures – as with the targeting of specific types or categories of transactions or the phased unwinding of sanctions or regulations. The use of the Sectoral Sanctions List in the Russia context, the restrictions on types of debt and equity sanctioned under that program, and the application of Section 311 against "bad banks" for a range of illicit financial activity are good examples of this type of creativity.

Juan Zarate
Financial Integrity Network

January 10, 2018

6. *Protecting the Integrity of the Financial System in Practice.* A core pillar of the current environment is the idea that the anti-money laundering/countering the financing of terrorism (AML/CFT) system and related measures are designed to protect the integrity of the financial system. This is a preventative model that over time has required greater transparency, accountability, and traceability within the financial system. Though imperfect in many ways, the effectiveness of the AML/CFT regime underlies the ability to use sanctions and other financial and economic measures to exclude rogue actors from the financial system. If sanctions screening is to work, banks and other regulated financial institutions must know their customer and understand ownership and control interests for entities using their facilities to transact around the world. These tools of financial exclusion must be balanced with demands and utility of financial inclusion. All of this requires Congress and the Administration to recognize that the tools of financial and economic coercion are highly dependent on the effectiveness of the AML/CFT regime and the integrity of the financial system. These disciplines are often treated as separate endeavors or even industries. In practice, they are two sides of the same coin with sanctions and AML/CFT blending ever more neatly in the age of conduct-based sanctions and the growing use of financial regulations like Section 311, which have the effect of sanctions.

7. *International Norm Setting, Cooperation, and Legitimacy.* The United States has the ability to impact globally with its financial and economic might -- the size and attractiveness of the U.S. economy, the role of the dollar as the chief reserve and trading currency, and the historic credibility and importance of U.S. authorities. This gives global reach to even unilateral U.S. measures. But the authority to sanction or exclude actors from the U.S. and global financial system should be used wisely, when possible in concert with other countries and institutions like the United Nations, and with a clear understanding with the private sector of the regulatory expectations. They should also be used while understanding and tending to the legal foundation of these measures along with serious concerns for privacy and civil liberties.

The long-term legitimacy of any action is dependent on whether financial and economic measures are taken in furtherance and in support of accepted international norms and can be supported by facts. The strength of our campaign to pressure Iran revolved around the isolation of suspect Iranian actors and the key sectors because of underlying prohibited or nefarious behavior in violation of international norms and sanctions – along with our ability to demonstrate to governments and private sector actors the real risks that Iran presented to the financial system. Prohibitions on support to terrorism, proliferation of weapons of mass destruction, money laundering, financial criminality, and corruption are all norms and requirements understood by legitimate actors in the public and private domains. Basing economic campaigns less on political decisions and diplomatic predilections and more on underlying conduct that affects both international security and the integrity of the financial system helps support the legitimacy of these actions. Continuing to set these norms, in cooperation with the major players in the global system and in organizations like the Financial Action Task Force, is essential to our effective use of these tools.

Juan Zarate
Financial Integrity Network

January 10, 2018

Urgency Attached to Effective Action

Ensuring the effective application and use of these measures is critical given the importance and complexity of these measures and the national security strategies affected. With the broadening and deepening of the application of sanctions to more conflicts, targets and types, and transnational conduct of concern – to include corruption, malicious cyber activity, and human rights violations – sustaining application with sufficient resources and policy attention becomes all the more important.

There is real urgency attached to this work. In the case of North Korea, there must be an all-out campaign to leverage financial information, sanctions, interdictions, and related financial measures to squeeze the regime's finances and access to capital. More importantly, these measures should be used to attempt to alter the dynamics with China by putting fundamental Chinese interests at risk – without needing to threaten China directly -- so they use their leverage to affect Pyongyang's decision-making.

This includes sanctioning entities – regardless of nationality or type – assisting North Korea to evade sanctions or engage in illicit or suspect financial or commercial activity; committing to a permanent and aggressive multi-national maritime interdiction campaign to address proliferation concerns, building off the Proliferation Security Initiative; deploying a multi-layered missile defense strategy that guards against missiles that can hit U.S. interests, allies, and U.S. territories, States, and the mainland; pursuing an aggressive anti-corruption/kleptocracy initiative to prosecute those profiting illegally or in violation of sanctions from dealings with Pyongyang and recovering any leadership-related assets; uncovering and designating those financially facilitating or profiting from human rights violations, cyber incursions, or proliferation activity. Other measures tied to monitoring of oil, coal, guest workers, and other trade proscribed under the current United Nations sanctions could tighten scrutiny and provide other avenues for enforcement actions. Under these conditions, it should be incredibly uncomfortable and fundamentally threatening for any country or entity to do business with Pyongyang.

With Iran, measures to isolate and pressure the Revolutionary Guard and the regime leadership – by spotlighting human rights abuses, corruption, support to terrorists and militant proxies, and the progress of their ballistic missile program in violation of UN sanctions – can be undertaken right away, regardless of one's view of the Joint Comprehensive Plan of Action (JCPOA) and would be consistent with that agreement's allowance for the application of non-nuclear sanctions.

With Russia, the United States must maintain escalatory dominance along with its European allies in the use of sanctions and economic statecraft – focusing ever more attention on Russia's continued aggression in Ukraine, Putin's corruption, support for Assad's regime in Syria and related human rights abuses, and malicious cyber activity. In the face of Russian use of its own economic and energy tools – along with its attempts to displace the U.S. dollar in the international financial system – the United States must maintain this pressure as a weapon of coercion, while being sensitive to European dependencies. Even if this does not roll back Russia's hold on Crimea, such measures should be used to deter further Russia aggression – in the physical and virtual worlds – against the United States and our allies.

Juan Zarate
Financial Integrity Network

In Venezuela, the use of sanctions to isolate the regime further by highlighting human rights abuses and corruption as the economy implodes and the regime descends further into dictatorship has to be handled with humanitarian designs squarely in mind to support the people.

With global terrorist organizations, continuing to apply financial pressure on the key dependencies and chokepoints for their financial infrastructure in the formal and informal system will be critical. This is especially the case for those terrorist groups, like Hizballah, which have a global, criminal footprint and a broad commercial and financial support mechanism.

And with transnational issues like proliferation finance, transnational organized crime, cyber hacking, and kleptocracy, where global financial networks support both illicit financial dealings and dangerous activity threatening to the United States, there is urgency to attacking the financial underpinnings that allow these networks to profit, connect dangerous actors, and undermine global security and governance.

There are many more programs and areas of focus, but in all of these campaigns, there is a need to ensure that the United States and its allies understand and can undermine the financial vulnerabilities of dangerous actors in the international system. Given the stakes, ensuring effectiveness of this system is all the more important now.

Improvement in Application of Sanctions and Financial Measures

There are certain overarching themes and issues that deserve focus if these financial measures are to remain effective and are to amplify the reach and sustainability of U.S. influence. These are arenas for improvement that apply to any and all uses of sanctions and financial measures.

- *Targeted, Strategic Enforcement.* To be effective, sanctions and financial measures must be enforced. Simply designating or labeling an activity of concern alone cannot ensure the effective application of sanctions or an effective campaign. This is essential as the targets of financial measures and actions grow more sophisticated and adapt around the pressure. Enforcement of sanctions evasion, anti-money laundering, and other financial criminal provisions allows authorities leeway to apply the criminal law, in addition to issuing regulations or sanctions in the wake of financial measures. This enforcement should ideally be coordinated, along with the inter-agency, while respecting the independence of relevant law enforcement and regulatory agencies. This does not preclude the use of targeting task forces and policy coordination at the federal level to ensure attention and enforcement on high-priority sanctions regimes and issues, along with consistency of approach in line with the U.S. government's strategy. There should be a tendency and default toward more enforcement task forces tied to strategic national security campaigns.

- *Focus on Ownership and Control.* The U.S. and European sanctions regimes explicitly cover ownership and control interests subject to sanctions for those designated under relevant sanctions programs. Regulated institutions are required to determine ownership and control interests for purposes of sanctions compliance based on percentages of

Juan Zarate
Financial Integrity Network

ownership and indicators of control or management, which are not often clear in the private sector. Though there is some attention by authorities to tracking and mapping ownership and control interests for designated parties, more needs to be done proactively and as a matter of consistent practice to investigate, analyze, and publish information about entities owned and controlled by designated parties.

This effort can take advantage of three trends in the environment: (1) greater attention to ownership/control requirements and disclosures under international standards, the Fourth EU Money Laundering Directive, and greater Office of Foreign Asset Control (OFAC) and regulatory attention in the United States; (2) the sensitivity in the private sector, beyond just the banking community, to understanding ownership interests for purposes of addressing corruption concerns and risks; and (3) the growing attention and work by commercial entities, think tanks, and advocacy groups in using open source data to compile network maps and lists of sanctioned parties' ownership interests. Groups like C4ADS, the Enough Project, and FDD have published and shared the names and identifiers of companies owned by designated parties or facilitating sanctions evasion. Treasury, through OFAC, should focus programmatically on enforcing follow-on sanctions on initial individual and network designations and explore ways of taking advantage appropriately of the open-source research and capabilities produced that could enable OFAC's research, follow-on designations, and enforcement.

- *More Aggressive Information Sharing Systems.* To understand better the risks and vulnerabilities to the financial system along with the economic infrastructure of those targeted, there needs to be a much more aggressive information sharing model that seeks to collect more targeted financial data while also allowing the private sector to share data more aggressively.

If the AML/CFT and sanctions system is to work, there needs to be a more aggressive and expansive information-sharing environment. In the first instance, this entails using regulatory authorities, like Geographic Targeting Orders, OFAC subpoenas, and Section 311 actions targeting "classes of transaction" to gather more financial and commercial data tied to sanctioned parties, jurisdictions, and their ownership and control interests. This idea allows for the use of financial regulation and legitimate and lawful information gathering tools to understand historical and shifting financial patterns and relationships, while helping the private sector focus on areas of prioritized concern and risk identified by U.S. authorities.

This also means taking advantage of public-private information sharing systems, like Section 314(a) of the USA PATRIOT Act, to focus collaboration on systemic and real vulnerabilities in key sectors. This moves beyond the classic Bank Secrecy Act system currently in place, and instead entails more targeted collaboration between regulated financial institutions, regulations, and law enforcement to target vulnerabilities and networks of concern. This happens episodically, is being piloted in specific projects, and in general is taking shape faster abroad. There needs to be a more aggressive model of cooperation between regulated financial entities and authorities in the United States.

Juan Zarate
Financial Integrity Network

This also means allowing global financial institutions the ability to share suspect account and transactional information across borders within their institutions. Currently, privacy and data protection laws in certain countries impede an institution's ability to share data within its own network or enterprise. Without this data, a financial institution may not see the risks and vulnerabilities in its own system without costly or time-consuming work-arounds. This is a 20th century model crashing against a 21st century economy and expectations. With illicit actors moving at the speed of the digital economy, these roadblocks to internal information sharing have to be overcome or removed.

Importantly, Section 314(b) of the Patriot Act must be expanded to allow financial institutions to share information within their respective sectors more consistently and rapidly. This requires that we begin to think about information sharing in the private sector as enabling the discovery of sector-wide vulnerabilities – like criminal networks that use multiple accounts at different institutions – as well as the effectiveness of our preventative measures against sector-wide risks. With the onset of new technologies that facilitate the collection of big data and predictive analytics, technology firms should help regulated industries create models that allow the private sector to share and analyze data more rapidly and effectively, while sharing the burden and costs of compliance. My partner, Chip Poncy, and I have written about moving toward a utility model for compliance risk management, which will save costs and manifest in different models as technology enables more effective data sharing, protection, and analysis.

- *Commitment to Reinforcing International Norms with Sanctions Campaigns.* The use of these tools must remain strategic, their implementation focused on effectiveness, and they must be reinforced with a strengthened and committed international system devoted to the protection of the international financial system and our collective security.

Indeed, one of the great strengths of the campaign to combat illicit finance is that it is based on international norms and principles that are subscribed to by all the relevant banking centers and jurisdictions – and that are now well understood by the private sector. These standards, established by the Financial Action Task Force and reinforced by the World Bank, International Monetary Fund (IMF), the United Nations, and countries around the world, form the baseline for the integrity of a financial system that is intended to be transparent, accountable, and safe. This also means that the sanctions system that has formed the core of these campaigns must be driven by the United States but adopted more fully by the legitimate capitals of the world. They must be encouraged to take on the task of combating illicit financing in their countries and globally.

In this regard, the United States has borne much of the burden (and often the blame) of enforcing sanctions intended to protect the financial system and the international community. It is Treasury's OFAC that produces the universal list of designated parties checked and screened against by all legitimate financial institutions in the world. There are no other jurisdictions that have a dedicated entity charged with enforcing sanctions, working with the private sector to provide guidance, or even defining how such authorities should be used on a consistent basis. This then lends itself to these tools being used internationally to settle political or diplomatic scores, instead of being technically

Juan Zarate
Financial Integrity Network

focused on isolating underlying illicit financial activity. There should be an international goal of professionalizing and institutionalizing the work of sanctions within the authorities of key banking and commercial centers around the world, which will aid in raising the level of effectiveness globally.

This is more important than ever as other countries begin to use sanctions and financial pressure campaigns outside the bounds of UN, U.S., or EU leadership for their own purposes – and with the norms, expectations, and boundaries of how aggressively these authorities can be used continuing to be shaped. This is especially the case with respect to the use of anti-corruption laws and sanctions, which are strategically critical and essential to deploy but can be misused by regime leadership to consolidate power and marginalize or bankrupt political adversaries.

This is also important as the United States and its allies find new partners, including non-state actors, who are aligned in their interest for financial integrity and the protection of the financial system. There are new partners in the international system who need to be enlisted as we combat new forms of illicit finance, and they can be enlisted more easily if the campaigns are attached to defending legitimate international norms.

For example, a new coalition could be galvanized to stop the funding of terror and conflict from the illicit wildlife trade – especially the decimation of elephants and rhinos in Africa for their valuable ivory. This trade, which will bring the extinction of some of the world's most magnificent animals, is exploited for profit by terrorist and militant actors, like al Shabaab, the Lord's Resistance Army, and the Janjaweed, along with drug trafficking organizations from South Asia and China. Treasury recently designated financial facilitators working with the Lord's Resistance Army to profit from this trade. The United States could help galvanize and energize additional international efforts to prevent these environmental crimes and focus a strategy on disrupting the financial and commercial networks that enable this trade to flourish. This effort would combine the environmental activists with the national security community. In this manner, we could serve both our natural and national security, with a new set of allies in the international system.

- *Targeted Unwinding.* The United States has grown incredibly sophisticated in the use of sanctions and financial measures to drive strategies of financial exclusion. Yet, as the Treasury and international community consider unwinding certain sanctions programs and delisting individuals and entities from longstanding sanctions lists, the United States should consider how best to manage targeted unwinding measures to achieve our strategic goals. Unwinding can occur because a change of behavior has been achieved, political or diplomatic goals met, or as a tool of continued persuasion. There are good and important reasons to unwind sanctions, but the way in which sanctions are unwound can reinforce our strategic goals and the influence of our financial measures.

Blunt unwinding may give a rogue regime too much in a deal, could reinforce the regime's hold on power and resources available to it, and may not allow for the targeting of relief to build the private sector or alternates sources of power or influence. It also may

Juan Zarate
Financial Integrity Network

not allow for steps – staged or targeted – that would force a regime to change its illicit financial behavior.

This is a challenge now with Iran and Cuba, and there are even lingering concerns with Burma. These are not just risky countries because they have fallen under sanctions. They are inherently suspect and present financial crimes risks because of the nature of their autocratic and corrupt economies, the opacity of their systems, and the use of the economy by the regimes for a range of dangerous or illicit activities.

A system of targeted unwinding could advance the strategic goal that an illicit regime or a network not misuse an economy and financial system to benefit terrorists, proxies, and accelerate its nefarious international ambitions and capabilities. It could also accelerate reforms that match international standards and expectations – and aid the local population. If such a system could prove effective, it might spur responsible reform within a country as it tries to reintegrate into the global system. The United States should ensure that it is using its power of unwinding to full effect in furtherance of its continued strategic goals.

- *Deploy Positive Economic Power.* With every financial exclusion strategy or campaign targeted at rogue actors, the U.S. government should devise a complementary strategy to leverage positive economic tools and greater financial inclusion to reward appropriate behavior and to support U.S. allies trying to do the right thing by complying with sanctions programs and financial measures. If human rights abusers are targeted with financial isolation, measures to support the cause and communications of human rights activists in that country or region should be supported. If corruption and kleptocratic regimes fall under the weight of a financial campaign, there should be financial benefits, regulatory relief, or investment incentives provided to market players willing to subscribe to the highest standards of anti-corruption practices and measures.

In addition, there is an argument for financial inclusion to serve as a national security imperative unto itself, to allow for greater transparency, improve economic development and prospects, and raise the level of compliance in developing and corrupt economies around the world. Governments have demanded that regulated financial communities serve as gatekeepers of the financial system, so as to ensure systems and institutions are not misused by criminal, sanctioned, or terrorist actors. Governments have equally been concerned that institutions, particularly major global banks, have exited from specific markets, business lines, and customers in reaction to perceived regulatory and real risk. The global banks have felt whipsawed by this dual message and pressure, while sectors such as money service businesses and certain communities have found themselves without banking services.

Where there is a need for financial services or international flows of funds, the international community should find a way of facilitating such flows. When those financial flows or transactions – as with remittances to and in conflict zones -- represent heightened and perhaps unmanageable sanctions and financial crime risk, then there

Juan Zarate
Financial Integrity Network

needs to be a shared solution to create safe corridors or channels for such financial activity.

If such flows are important to unstable economies or remittance-dependent countries, then governments and international financial institutions, like the IMF and World Bank, need to devise ways to build comfort in the risks that can be taken by providing safe channels for flows or helping to validate ecosystems of financial transparency that meet acceptable international standards. No system is perfect, and in a risk-based AML/CFT model there is an acceptance of a certain degree of risk. Without some public sector or international assumption of risk, the private sector will avoid environments that present costly and unjustifiable risk. The twin goals of financial integrity and inclusion can be met with some creative collaboration.

Challenges Ahead

There are enormous challenges to the ability of the United States to use the tools of economic coercion to drive its national security goals, starting with the nature and complexity of the targets themselves to direct challenges to the American economic order.

The Blending of Illicit Financial Networks

Importantly, money allows seemingly disparate networks and groups to blend their operations and facilitate their activities. Money – and the potential for profit – grease relationships that would ordinarily never exist. This adaptive collaboration is seen already in the case of drug trafficking, where groups like Hizballah and al Qaida in the Islamic Maghreb (AQIM) have profited from the drug trade from South America through West Africa and the Sahel into Europe. In the past, al Qaida and groups like Lashkar-e-Taiba (LeT) have benefited from alliances with Indian crime lord Dawood Ibrahim and his organized crime network. The overlaps between the criminal underworld, illicit financial activity, and terrorist operations and funding will continue to evolve as marriages of convenience emerge in common areas of operation. Focusing on key financial conduits, nodes, and networks that serve not just terrorists but transnational criminals will be critical for counterterrorism officials.

This principle of opportunistic profit and operations is now implicating the interactions of networks of all ideological stripes. There is money to be made and logistical networks to be harnessed to achieve criminal and political goals.

This blend of purposes is seen most clearly in the conversion of terrorist groups into drug trafficking organizations – like the FARC in Colombia, the Taleban in Afghanistan, and Lebanese Hizballah. With Hizballah, the U.S. government continues to expose the connections between the group and international drug trafficking and money laundering. Recent actions by the Drug Enforcement Administration (DEA) and Treasury to dismantle networks of Hizballah's "Business Affairs Component" have exposed financial and trade nodes that the Hizballah operates and led to arrests and enforcement actions around the world. Treasury's Section 311 action against Lebanese Canadian Bank (LCB) in 2011 exposed the hundreds of millions of

Juan Zarate
Financial Integrity Network

January 10, 2018

dollars Hizballah was moving as part of its drug money laundering scheme globally. Overall, the U.S. government has designated Hizballah supporters in twenty countries around the world.

Ideology gives way to opportunity. The reason is money. America's enemies – drug trafficking cartels, organized crime groups, militant groups, and terrorists -- are funding each other, as a matter of convenience and opportunity.

These connections also tie groups together and allow them to work together more broadly. The DEA, the Federal Bureau of Investigation, and the intelligence community have focused more and more attention on the nexus between drugs and terror – with terrorist groups assuming the role of drug trafficking organizations and drug trafficking organizations taking on the characteristics and violent methodologies of terrorist groups. The U.S. Attorney for the Southern District of New York has merged its international drug and foreign terrorism sections because of the intimate link between the two.

Crime can pay, making it an especially attractive avenue for fundraising for networks and groups with global ambitions. Where there is money to be made and moved, financial institutions will be implicated. Banks and financial intermediaries will continue to weigh the balance between making significant amounts of money while doing business with suspect customers and the need to apply the most stringent financial controls and standards on money flowing through its systems. We have seen this over and over, with multinational banks targeted by regulatory authorities and investigators for taking chances with their efforts to evade sanctions and scrutiny.

Growing Sophistication & Illicit Financing Channels

Illicit financial networks continue to grow in sophistication and take advantage of the international financial system to profit and move money. Sophisticated organized crime groups and drug cartels use the same channels in the international financial and commercial systems to build their financial empires. Drugs, illicit goods, and money all flow, and facilitators and illicit money managers help devise ways to hide and layer transactions and evade scrutiny.

The Panama Papers leaks reveal how corporate vehicles formed by Mossack Fonseca were used by some, like Rami Makhlouf (the cousin of Bashar al Assad), and the former Qaddafi regime, to evade sanctions and move and hide millions of dollars in wealth. The arrest of "King Midas," the chief money launderer for the Sinaloa cartel in Mexico revealed an intricate network of financial interests that allowed him to handle and hide nearly $4 billion over ten years for the organization, according to press accounts. Treasury actions – to include the Section 311 action against Banca Privada d'Andorra – revealed intricate schemes run by third-party money launderers to move money for clients in Venezuela, Russia, and China. And FinCEN's Geographic Targeting Order for high-value real estate purchases in New York and Miami – especially through shell companies -- is an attempt to gather information about a real money laundering vulnerability in the United States.

In many cases, the old methodologies of money laundering and tax evasion are refreshed, with greater awareness of the controls in place through regulation and financial due diligence. Sanctions evasion blends seamlessly into other financial crimes like tax evasion and money

Juan Zarate
Financial Integrity Network

laundering. Some money launderers have learned how to game banks' compliance systems and work around existing sanctions and financial crime controls.

New technologies and innovations in the storage and movement of money and value are reshaping the international financial landscape. This is especially the case in developing economies and communities without access to formal financial outlets, which are relying more heavily on mobile devices and mechanisms for storing and transferring money. The pace of growth of these systems in the developing world has been staggering. By 2009, the developing world accounted for three-quarters of the more than four billion mobile handsets in use. Prepaid cards, as an alternate way to store and transfer value, have gained momentum over the years as a replacement for standard currency transactions, with more innovation on the horizon. Crowd sourcing and fundraising facilitated by social media and the Internet – a problem anticipated by a Treasury Department report issued in 2003 – are now a regular means by which terrorist groups raise and move money.

In addition, the development of online, alternative currencies and new mechanisms for virtual barter will further open the Internet for potential exploitation by illicit actors. The Liberty Reserve and Silk Road networks demonstrated the rapid evolution of digital illicit marketplaces where all forms of illicit goods and activities – drugs, arms, and human trafficking – were blended and facilitated by digital currencies. The Department of Justice and FinCEN's actions against BTC-e, a foreign digital currency exchange for money laundering, is an other example of growing scrutiny from U.S. authorities on the flows of illicit funds through cryptocurrencies and exchanges.

Authorities must continue to worry about the crypto-economy facilitating access to illicit capital. But digital currencies and underlying technologies and applications have emerged as efficient ways to store value, reduce payment friction, lower costs of transactions, and enable more people to interact directly and securely. Major global banks are now investing in new FinTech ventures and experimenting with the use of blockchain technologies for classic banking functions like cross-border payments. Central Banks are now considering whether and how to develop and deploy national digital currencies. All the while, new currencies, apps, and financial functionality are emerging on the digital scene, competing to create an ecosystem of digital commerce.

Tracking the mass volumes of rapid and anonymous money flows around the world and getting in front of new technologies to allow for lawful and appropriate tracking will remain major challenges for law enforcement, intelligence, and regulatory officials, especially because groups and individuals are able to hide and layer their identities and ownership interests.

In this context, regulators, policymakers, and enforcement agencies will need to understand better how these new technologies work and are evolving, how they may be helpful in uncovering illicit behavior, and how to distinguish between legitimate actors seeking to comply with the law and those trying to evade all scrutiny and facilitate illicit activity. They must do this in a rapidly changing environment where innovation should not be squelched and where illicit activity cannot be ignored. With the rapid increase in value and attention to bitcoin, the growing interest in "Initial Coin Offerings," and deeper investments and interest in blockchain

Juan Zarate
Financial Integrity Network

technologies and platforms, authorities will need to devise strategies to apply the principles of financial integrity and security in this environment.

The technology sector will need to work more closely with government agencies around the world to help inform regulators, standard setters, and investigators about how new technologies and innovations work. The private sector will need to design new models for the use of technologies like blockchain and digital currencies that enable financial inclusion, traceability, lower payment friction and costs, and enable accountability for transactions. Some of this is already happening in the marketplace. The private sector – technology companies, investors, and companies leveraging these new capabilities -- should take ownership together of designing technologies, platforms, and protocols that help solve the conundrum of needing to ensure security, transparency, and accountability with technologies created to deepen anonymity.

Systemic Weaknesses

The international environment for financial integrity has matured rapidly. There are now clear international standards and heightened expectations for transparency and accountability, with the definition of financial crime expanding to include issues like tax evasion along with the broadened use of financial sanctions to address national security risks. The sanctions and anti-money laundering worlds have begun to blend with expectations that the financial and commercial communities take ownership of managing the real risks to their institutions. Jurisdictions too are now being judged by the effectiveness of their AML/CFT and sanctions systems. Though expectations are high, performance has fallen short and the global effort to protect the integrity of the financial system has proven imperfect and often ineffective.

The Panama and Paradise Papers revealed systemic weaknesses that have been understood by experts for some time. The leaks have revealed to the public what was already known to many of us. There are corners of the international financial system – in some jurisdictions, certain institutions, and in specific sectors – that have not received the light of international scrutiny and attention. Corporate formation agents and facilitators have often operated under the cloak of bank secrecy or lack of regulation. Investment advisors have not been subjected previously to regulation or scrutiny. Some lawyers have acted as financial facilitators, planners, and conduits for illicit activity. The gatekeepers of significant financial activity have taken advantage of the opacity of corporate structures and often been exempted from anti-money laundering regulation.

This is why the Treasury's Customer Due Diligence (CDD) rule, requiring financial institutions to verify the ultimate beneficial owners of companies, is a critical and important step in creating greater transparency in the system. This is also why proposed legislation requiring companies to know and file information on their ultimate beneficial owners is a critical next step to ensure that U.S. companies are not being used by international criminals and sanctions evaders to hide or move illicit capital and investments.

The United States must remain committed to its own financial transparency. Our economy cannot be seen or used as a money-laundering conduit or haven for illicit actors of any stripe. We need the transparency envisioned in the recently published CDD rule and the proposed beneficial ownership legislation. This will entail demanding similar transparency and regulation in

Juan Zarate
Financial Integrity Network

jurisdictions around the world, including those emerging as major economies or out from under sanctions.

The United States must continue to enforce sanctions and its financial crimes and anti-corruption laws to ensure that financial security threats are being addressed. The United States has consistently been the driver in using its toolkit to expose terrorist and criminal networks, and its work to enforce anti-corruption laws has resulted in global impact, as seen in the FIFA corruption cases. The United States should not be shy in driving enforcement, as long as it is justified by the facts and clearly intended to meet the demands of the U.S. legal system and international norms. It should also ask the same of its partners, especially the enforcement of sanctions.

Systemically, there are some additional worrying signs. In Europe, the legal structure and basis for the use of targeted sanctions against individuals and entities, based on United Nations designations, remains under enormous stress. The need to reconcile ex-ante due process for individuals with the preventative demands of asset freezes and designations continues to challenge the mechanism by which the European Union adopts and enforces targeted sanctions. Without a solid foundation and a sustainable system, the European Union and countries will remain reluctant to adopt aggressive measures to stop terrorist financing using these tools.

In addition, the ecosystem that allows for this form of financial warfare and isolation is resilient but fragile. The forced isolation of more and more actors – and the tendency of the private sector to decline doing business in at-risk sectors, jurisdictions, and with suspect actors – raises the possibility of reaching a tipping point where the effectiveness of these tools begins to diminish. This is especially the case when the use of financial sanctions and regulations are used to address a more diverse range of diplomatic and political ills and concerns – like human smuggling, child labor, and human rights abuses.

With the threat of financial sanctions, public opprobrium, and the potential erosion of reputation for banking suspect actors, legitimate financial actors have exited or stayed away from problematic markets. This raises concerns that less credible or scrupulous financial actors will fill the vacuum. It further raises the concern that legitimate and credible financial institutions will abandon markets most in need of access to capital and an improved culture of compliance and an embedding of global standards across the board. For authorities, this would entail a potential loss of visibility into certain financial activity.

We have seen this happening already – with banks stung by enforcement actions and painful, public settlements beginning to exit markets and business lines wholesale, money service businesses in North America struggling to find banking relationships with major banks, and embassies searching to maintain bank accounts in the United States and Switzerland.

An inherent and dynamic tension has emerged between the isolation of suspect behavior from the formal financial system and the incorporation of more of the world into the formal financial system. Going forward, the core principle of isolating and exiling actors from the legitimate financial system for policymakers needs to be seen as complementary to the need to expand the

Juan Zarate
Financial Integrity Network

January 10, 2018

reach and capabilities of the legitimate financial system to manage and address illicit financing risks.

More worrisome, our ability to use these powers could diminish as the economic landscape changes. Treasury's power ultimately stems from the ability of the United States to use its financial powers with global effect. This ability, in turn, derives from the centrality and stability of New York as a global financial center, the importance of the dollar as a reserve currency, and the demonstration effects of any steps, regulatory or otherwise, taken by the United States in the broader international system.

If the U.S. economy loses its predominance, or the dollar sufficiently weakens, our ability to wage financial warfare against terrorists and America's enemies could wane. It is vital that policymakers and ordinary Americans understand what is at stake and how this new brand of financial warfare evolved. For it is only a matter of time until U.S. competitors use the lessons of the past decade to wage financial battles of their own—especially against the United States.

Addressing the Convergence of Cyber and Financial Warfare

The frequency and sophistication of attacks on banks are increasing, with each attack representing a more dangerous intrusion and demonstration of systemic vulnerabilities. The recent attacks on the SWIFT system were a wake-up call for the international community that the systemic vulnerabilities are real. CitiBank alone reports ten million cyber attacks on its system a month. Banks are prime targets for sophisticated, organized cyber criminals. Banks hold not just money and customer accounts, but also collect and centralize sensitive customer data and some clients' intellectual property.

More importantly, banks have been pulled into a more serious and sustained cyber financial battle. Nation states and their proxies realize that banks serve as both key systemic actors important for the functioning of the global economy and as chief protagonists in the isolation of rogue regimes and actors from the financial system. Thus, the financial community finds itself drawn into combined financial and cyber battles – neither of which it controls. This has led cyber security experts in the banking community to admit openly, "We are at war."

Western banks and the financial system are now encountering the convergence between economic and cyber warfare. Major and minor state powers, along with super-empowered individuals and networks, can harness economic interdependence and cyber weapons to increase their global power status at the expense of their geopolitical rivals. The danger emerging is a coalition of actors – perhaps states using non-state proxies in cyber space -- launching financial and cyber assaults.

The need for urgent attention to this convergence within the financial community and among Washington policymakers is clear. The current level of interaction between stakeholders is not sufficient to address the growing threat from cyber financial attacks. There needs to be a more aggressive approach to private sector defense of its systems and public-private collaboration to defend critical financial systems.

Juan Zarate
Financial Integrity Network

January 10, 2018

This approach would borrow in part from the post 9/11 anti-money laundering and sanctions model to leverage financial suasion against rogue capital and actors as a way of protecting the financial system. President Obama's April 1, 2015 Executive Order allowing for the use of sanctions to address malicious cyber activity is an important cornerstone to this approach and related cyber financial deterrence. This would also entail a more aggressive "cyber privateering" model to empower and enlist the private sector to better defend its systems in coordination with the government.

We need to begin to address the convergence of cyber and financial warfare as the leading front in systemic vulnerabilities to the integrity and safety of the international financial system.

A Comprehensive U.S. National Economic Strategy

Ultimately, sanctions and financial measures cannot be viewed in isolation and cannot be assumed to be the province of the United States alone. As noted above, the tools and the strategies of financial exclusion need to be embedded in broader strategies of national and economic security. The United States and the international community have begun to wrestle with the complications of an interconnected global environment where economic power, access to resources, and cutting-edge technologies are redefining national power. The myriad vulnerabilities and opportunities in this shifting landscape require a new national economic security strategy. The President's new National Security Strategy begins to address this new landscape and the need to focus on national economic security.

For many years, countries such as China and Russia had been playing a new geo-economic game, where all forms of economic power are leveraged aggressively for national advantage. In this vein, the United States should concentrate on sharpening its tools and reinforcing the strength and resilience of a transparent international financial system, along with its partners. This should not just be a strategy of financial exclusion.

The United States should find ways to develop strategies of financial inclusion, using its economic influence, private investment, and commercial interests abroad to help allies, reinforce strategic interests, and complement the strategies of financial exclusion. Good behavior and allies around the world should be rewarded with investment and opportunities to work with the United States and our private sector, and U.S. economic tools should not be seen as simply confined to the quiver of economic sanctions.

Importantly, the United States should develop defensive economic strategies with our allies to counter the potential influence and pressure that countries like Russia and China may wield. International alliances should be recast to ensure key resource and supply redundancy, while trade deals should create new opportunities for influence and economic advantage. The United States should deploy new doctrines of deterrence like a "boomerang deterrent" making it patently unwise for countries to try to attack or weaken the U.S. given the entanglement of the international commercial and financial systems.

The U.S. government's approach to its economic vulnerabilities is also scattered – with strategies to protect supply chain security, combat transnational organised crime, secure the cyber domain,

Juan Zarate
Financial Integrity Network

January 10, 2018

protect critical infrastructure, and promote U.S. private sector interests abroad to compete with state-owned enterprises. As the Venn diagram of economic and national security overlaps ever more exactly, the U.S. should craft a deliberate strategy that aligns economic strength with national security interests more explicitly and completely. It should also design this strategy with its allies squarely in mind.

The intelligence community should prioritise collection and analysis to focus on the global landscape through this lens. The Departments of Commerce, Energy, and Defense should sit down together – and then with the private sector – to determine how to maintain investments and access to strategic materials and capabilities critical to national security. Our homeland security enterprise should focus on protecting and building redundancies in the key infrastructure and digital systems essential for national survival. Law enforcement and regulators should have access to beneficial ownership information for suspect investments and companies formed in the United States.

Congress and the Administration should also review the traditional divide between the public and private sectors where cooperation is essential. We should view the relationship between government agencies – such as the Export-Import Bank, Overseas Private Investment Corporation (OPIC), and USAID – and businesses as core to the promotion of U.S. interests, creating alliances based not just on trade and development but also on shared economic vulnerabilities and opportunities. The White House needs to ensure that its national security and economic experts are sitting at the same table crafting and driving the strategy while consulting the private sector.

In doing this, U.S. and Western liberal democracies must reaffirm their core principles. Western capitalist societies should not strive to be like either China or Russia, and analysts should not automatically overestimate the strength of such alternate systems and inadvertently create structures that move us towards a state authoritarian model. On the contrary, the United States should commit to remaining the vanguard of the global free trade, capitalist system, while preserving the independence of the private sector and promoting ethical American business practices. The United States and its allies should not retreat from the globalised environment they helped shape, but instead take full advantage of the innovation and international appeal of American and Western business and technology.

In the twenty-first century, economic security underpins the nation's ability to project its power and influence. The United States must remain true to its values, but start playing a new, deliberate game of geo-economics to ensure its continued security and strength.

The power to affect the budgets of America's enemies is an enormous power that needs to be tended carefully and wielded wisely. America's enemies – especially nimble and sophisticated actors enabled by nation states -- will continue to find ways to work around the international pressure and strictures put on them. These are delicate but essential tools that if tended properly will continue to form a key part of American power projection and part of the international architecture to protect both the international financial system and security.

Thank you again for the privilege of testifying.

Chairman ROYCE. Thank you, Mr. Zarate.

Mr. Maltz.

STATEMENT OF MR. DEREK MALTZ, EXECUTIVE DIRECTOR, GOVERNMENTAL RELATIONS, PEN-LINK, LTD. (FORMER SPECIAL AGENT IN CHARGE, SPECIAL OPERATIONS DIVISION, DRUG ENFORCEMENT ADMINISTRATION, U.S. DEPARTMENT OF JUSTICE)

Mr. MALTZ. Chairman Royce and distinguished members of the committee, I would like to thank you for this opportunity to discuss these important topics for our national security.

Chairman Royce, after hearing the news this week, I want to echo Juan's comment. I wanted to congratulate you and your family for an outstanding career in public service and all you have done for our Nation.

And I know firsthand, as Juan already alluded to, that you were very much the leader behind helping us get Viktor Bout, and put him in jail, and take him out of the battle space. So thank you in words, not action—I am sorry, action, not words, Congressman.

Chairman ROYCE. Thanks, Derek.

Mr. MALTZ. I was the agent in charge at the Special Operations Division for almost 10 years and I am in daily contact with all my friends in law enforcement around the globe. I am very focused in on the threats to this country and how they impact our national security.

As you remember, I lost my brother Michael in the U.S. Air Force Pararescue unit in Afghanistan. So I am extremely passionate about public safety and national security and accountability. My days at SOD, I witnessed tremendous successes, unbelievable workers. My last success was when El Chapo Guzman was captured by the Mexican authorities based on a total U.S. interagency success. So I was very, very excited about that.

But we will never be safe in this country unless we get 100 percent full information sharing. I know that is kind of like a stretch to try to get 100 percent, but we could do a lot better. We need everyone on the same page, and that is to keep America safe. Everyone has equities, but we have to have them on the same page.

The topic of unity effort has been my priority ever sense I buried my brother and will continue to be until I am done. And that means that I am going to try hard to unite the people, not divide them.

I watched this threat grow all the years in the Special Operations Division, but luckily I got some good support and we expanded the operation from 9 to 30 agencies, to include our partners in the NYPD who are out there on the front lines every day trying to protect us.

I remain committed to work with Congress, this committee, and I want to help provide recommendations and solutions. I don't want to be the doom-and-gloom guy that is just going to just keep bothering people and kind of blaming people.

We can't beat these sophisticated criminal networks working in silos. We have myopic views at times in this country. And people are working very, very hard. So we want to put it all together. We want synergy.

With the latest controversy in the news regarding Project Cassandra and the DEA's multiagency operation against Hezbollah, let me make this clear. I want to offer suggestions, and I hope that Project Cassandra and the terror cases can result in productive discussions to develop better ways ahead.

I would like to see our dedicated men and women in law enforcement, the intelligence community, and DOD come together in attacking Hezbollah. The government already has a solid transnational organized crime strategy. When are we going to put it into action and hold people accountable?

The government has been looking at this for many years. This isn't rocket science, right? These are bad guys trying to destroy our way of life. Now we have to go after them in unity. We need to carry out President Trump's executive order and push hard against these biggest threats.

I really don't believe it is productive to start playing the blame game and wasting time going back and forth, criticizing the past administration. We have to be more effective in the future. The threats to this country are moving at lightning speed and we need more of a sense of urgency.

There is an old saying: Opportunities come and go. Well, in my personal opinion, having been the guy in charge of the Special Operations for 10 years, we lost a golden opportunity to crush Hezbollah. And that is what we want to do.

And the guys and ladies in the law enforcement community and the other agencies are doing this job right now as we sit here today. So we need to support them and give them the resources. It makes no sense to play that political ping-pong game going back and forth because no one is going to win and the bad guys are going to win.

So let's look at the mud that they are stuck in with the politics and the bureaucracy and let's start bringing people together. That is what we need to do.

Terrorists are going to continue to tap into the unbelievable funding streams of criminal activities. One case after another we see this. But we still have our terror investigators and our crime investigations going down two separate paths. We need to break down the walls. Who is going to do it? Who is going to step up and do it?

We can't be effective if we don't eliminate these walls. We need the AG, the DHS secretary, the DOD leaders, the intelligence community, committees like this to step up and tell people what they are going to do and what they are expected to do for the public. Let's make a commitment to the taxpayers that we are going to eliminate these barriers.

Let's build up capabilities like these sanctions, because Viktor Bout would probably still be out there if it wasn't for the sanctions. We exposed him, we created a vulnerability, and then law enforcement came and took him off the playing field, right?

So, sadly, 16 years after 9/11, we are still talking about information sharing. It is a disaster. We have to stop it. Terrorists are ruthless criminals and they are looking to destroy our way of life. We are not going to stop it with just DOD engagement, sanctions, and intelligence collection. We need robust law enforcement prosecutions, pursuant to the rule of law, to bring these people back to face justice and get full debriefings. The American people expect us to do this.

We need action and a sense of urgency. Thanks to this committee, I think we are going to be on the right path.

We need to have a mutually supportive framework so the IC equities and the law enforcement equities are all met.

The poor families awoke to the news of the 241 Americans that were killed in Beirut 34 years ago, right? Admiral Stavridis, General Kelly, they have been testifying for years about this emerging threat. How many more warning signs do we need? Michael Chertoff said they made al-Qaeda look like the minor leagues. I mean, what are we doing? We have to wake up and go after them hard. We are missing the accountability piece.

So what I would like to see is: Who is responsible in the U.S. Government to be accountable for these interagency task forces? Who is going to make sure that American interests are protected? Not any one agency. So that is what I would like to see. There has got to be open and collaborative efforts.

In my view, the worst thing the country needs now is to spend taxpayers' money on another coordination center when we have a facility sitting out in northern Virginia, right here in our backyard, with 30 agencies, 3 countries. There are probably more than 30 agencies now. We need to stop the madness, and I am going to help try to do that in my capacity.

Cannot stand alone. Sanctions cannot stand alone, all right? They have to be applied and enforced. Your statement—and I am done, I promise—only as strong as the enforcement, right? The same thing in these strategies. You can write strategies all day long. Who is enforcing the strategies? Because they are good strategies.

Thank you very much.

[The prepared statement of Mr. Maltz follows:]

Since most of the relevant agencies are already represented at SOD and the entity follows the rule of law under the guidance of the Department of Justice, it would be a great place to bring people together the nation's best and brightest to crush the sophisticated and growing threats. There should be a resource allocation review and we need all the agencies to contribute valuable personnel that can work in a cohesive team.

In my 28 years in law enforcement, I've seen many operations that were both successful and failures. Many of the failures that I have witnessed were not a result of lack of effort or skill by the investigators. Rather, those failures were the result of lack of leadership and political infighting that created an environment built around securing and maintaining one's own kingdom, as opposed to serving the American people. I believe that if the U.S.G. would implement some of the recommendations in this document, we can make this country a safer place for current and future generations.

OPERATIONAL FOCUS:

We can have all the strategies and plans in the world, but without accountability and operational implementation, the U.S.G. will fall further being in the fight against TOC networks. Project Cassandra was a successful investigation in many aspects, coordinated by SOD, a multi- agency operational coordination center with 30 agencies represented, and it led to unprecedented results and exposed elements of the terrorist group Hezbollah who were being funded by worldwide cocaine sales. There were also many other criminal investigations coordinated at SOD assisting the field investigators around the globe while providing valuable intelligence to the IC and the DOD.

During 2008, the U.S. cooperative investigation with Colombia culminated with over 130 arrests, to include many of the senior-level operatives, and $23 million was seized. (Rotella, 2008) This case identified the scope and the alliance between South American drug traffickers to money laundering operations in Hong Kong, Central America, Africa and Canada, and a connection to several Lebanese criminals associated with a global organized crime network.

Based on the substantial information developed during this phase of Cassandra and very alarming and emerging trends exposed, the Counter-Narco Terrorism Operations Center (CNTOC) located at SOD commenced an initiative focusing on all aspects of this network. The CNTOC has representatives from numerous agencies to ensure that information collected and analyzed can be immediately passed to the appropriate agencies and that the agencies can work in a collaborative task force environment.

The CNTOC spearheaded a focused investigation with the field offices on the Middle Eastern money launderers working with the South American drug traffickers who were shipping multi-ton quantities of cocaine into West Africa for distribution around the world. During this initiative, DEA identified the leader of this sophisticated network who coordinated multi-ton shipments of cocaine from Colombia to Los Zeta's Mexican Drug Cartel and was laundering hundreds of millions of dollars in drug proceeds back to Colombia. The main operative also established a very sophisticated network in West Africa to move currency via couriers back to Lebanon.

The CNTOC organized a four-phased plan to include OFAC designations against substantial targets, identified as Ayman Joumaa, Elissa and Ayash Exchange, a USA Patriot

Act 311 action against Lebanese Canadian Bank, a civil money laundering action against Lebanese Canadian Bank and Hezbollah's used car businesses involved in the scheme and criminal prosecution directed at the leaders of the Hezbollah involved with the drug and money laundering operation. CNTOC's strategy attempted to include all the tools of national power in a focused effort to disrupt and dismantle this trade-based money-laundering scheme. Unfortunately there were some agencies that did not participate or cooperate so the unity of effort wasn't successful.

In January 2011, the Office of Foreign Assets Control (OFAC) of the Department of Treasury, under the specially designated narcotics traffickers kingpin program, designated ten individuals and twenty entities related to the Joumaa organization to include the Elissa and Ayash Exchanges in Lebanon. (Center, Treasury Targets Major Lebanese-Based Drug Trafficking and Money Laundering Network , 2011)

In February 2011, The Department of Treasury with DEA announced the identification of the Lebanese Canadian Bank (LCB) as a financial institution of primary money-laundering concern under section 311 of the USA Patriot Act. **This was the first time ever** the 311 Action was used in a drug case. The organized crime network was moving large shipments of drugs from South America to Europe and the Middle East via West Africa and laundering hundreds of millions of dollars to accounts held at LCB as well as through trade base money-laundering involving consumer goods throughout the world, including used car dealerships in the U.S. LCB was helping Hezbollah through the Joumaa network. (Center, Treasury Identifies Lebanese Canadian Bank Sal as a "Primary Money Laundering Concern", 2011)

Subsequently in December 2011, there was a complaint filed in the Southern District of New York exposing this Lebanese money-laundering scheme which investigators documented over $300 million into United States for the purchase and shipment of used cars to West Africa. The complaint alleged that the assets of LCB, Hassan Ayash Exchange and Elissa Holding, along with the assets of approximately 30 U.S. car buyers and a U.S. shipping company and related entities that facilitate the scheme, are forfeitable as the proceeds of violations of the International Emergency Economic Powers Act (IEEPA).

Through this investigation, the task force of agencies exposed the LCB as money-laundering for Hezbollah through a very aggressive financial attack against the network. The elaborate scheme exposed very innovative ways terrorist groups like Hezbollah could identify alternate sources of income to fund their operations. As terrorists are increasingly turning to criminal networks for their funding, this operation clearly supported this statement made by the President of the United States and Senior Homeland Security Officials. This particular complaint was seeking penalties totaling $483 million. From January 1, 2007 to early 2011 at least $329 million was transferred by wire from LCB and the two exchange houses and other financial institutions for the purchase and shipment of used cars. (DEA, DEA News: Civil Suit Exposes Lebanese, 2011)

During the December 2011 time frame, the Eastern District of Virginia announced the indictment of Ayman Joumaa for coordinating the shipment of tens of thousands of kilograms of cocaine from Colombia to Los Zetas Drug Cartel for distribution into the United States over an eight year period. Joumaa was also charged with laundering millions of dollars in drug proceeds for the organization. Joumaa's organization was further exposed through the OFAC sanction. (EDVA, 2011)

Subsequent to the lawsuit against the LCB, investigators revealed that the LCB personnel moved assets to other banks in Lebanon in a way to hide the assets from the United States government. This criminal activity was part of the international scheme where several Lebanese financial institutions with connections to Hezbollah used the U.S. banks to launder narcotics proceeds through West Africa into Lebanon. In August 2012, the Southern District of New York filed a 981K action against five corresponding banks in the United States that were doing business with Banque Labano Francais. This particular Lebanese bank received $150 million from the Lebanese Canadian bank after they were exposed with their international money-laundering business.

As a result of this very successful 981K action, the Banque Labano Francais, transferred $150 million to the United States Marshals Service account in New York. In June 2013, the Southern District of New York settled a civil forfeiture action against the Lebanese Canadian bank and the settlement required LCB to forfeit $102 million to the United States. This was an unprecedented action targeting Hezbollah and their worldwide illicit activities. The settlement also identified to the world that international money-launderers for terrorists and narco-traffickers will face serious consequences even when the activity is outside the US (Justice, 2012) (York, 2013)

During February 2016, DEA working with European law enforcement identified a massive Hezbollah drug and money-laundering scheme. This complex investigation targeted Hezbollah's Lebanese Hezbollah's Business Affairs Component (LHBAC). This particular component has been engaged in weapons purchases for   Hezbollah to support its activities in Syria. This investigation involved multiple countries and showed once again the connection between Hezbollah and drug trafficking. This particular aspect focused on LHBAC. The LHBAC formed a business relationship with the South American cocaine traffickers responsible for shipping multi-tons of cocaine around the world. The massive proceeds made by this element provides proceeds for the purchase of weapons needed for their international terrorist operations. (DEA, DEA and European Authorities Uncover Massive Hezbollah Drug and Money Laundering Scheme, 2016)

RECOMMENDATIONS MOVING FORWARD:

- One of my main recommendations would be to take the foundation of what has been created at SOD with the several supporting intelligence centers, OCDETF Fusion Center, CBP's NTC, DOD's NTC and others in the beltway, and enhance the interagency efforts by adding important financial investigative resources.
- We need to utilize the powerful criminal laws of the United States of America and prosecute and extradite the significant members of the organizations.
- The basic principle that needs to be enforced to keep America safe is 100% Information sharing. The DOJ needs to maintain the leadership, oversight and responsibility for the multi-agency project since they are responsible for the ultimate prosecution. The Center needs to be adequately staffed and resources. FBI and HSI should elevate the leadership within the center for maximum "unity of effort" and "buy in" from their field operatives and management.

- Since Crime and Terror overlap and we have identified several global fund raising schemes that are crossing into the criminal investigations, we need to break down the walls and legal impediments, and develop sound sharing processes. We need to enhance the existing Global Threat Finance Teams with the expertise to disrupt and dismantle the financial aspects of these networks using all the powerful U.S. Treasury Actions.
- We should not duplicate efforts and initiate the creation of any new coordination centers in the beltway. This would most likely be a waste of resources, and would result in a significant setback. We must build on what we already have instead of causing confusion for the field investigators.
- We need a team designated at DOJ for high value transnational organized crime extraditions to ensure we don't miss opportunities like in Project Cassandra. From past experience we know the intelligence value for all of the U.S.G. agencies when we debrief high value subjects so we can't lose this capability.
- I believe that by placing qualified personnel in key leadership positions with law enforcement background at SOD, we can ensure that communication is flowing appropriately in both directions between law enforcement and the other pertinent agencies.
- As terrorists are looking for funding to carry out their dangerous agendas, criminal activity has been a golden source of revenue. This means, the agencies need to "break down the barriers" and unite. In the year 2018, it's almost impossible to successfully investigate global terrorists without utilizing the amazing criminal law enforcement personnel around the globe. It should be "one great U.S.G. force". We need to unite not divide.
- Since terrorist groups are tapping into criminal enterprises to help fund and facilitate activities, leadership must support and advance the multi-agency successful efforts of groups like the CNTOC and form stronger connectivity with the FBI's Joint Terrorism Task Forces.
- We need to continue building advanced technical capabilities within law enforcement agencies so they can stay with the criminal networks who are always looking of new ways to use technology to thwart law enforcement operations.
- A multi-agency group from Homeland Security, Justice Department, IC and DOD should examine operations like Project Cassandra to develop best practices to move forward. The complex transnational organized crime groups are constantly evolving and becoming more sophisticated.
- Law enforcement and the intelligence community need to form closer alliances. A unified effort is a must. They must place some of the best and brightest people into positions like the CNTOC and continue to pursue the sophisticated groups in a focused and prioritized manner. If you successfully crush a criminal organization's financial network, you will significantly increase the chances of disrupting their illicit activities. This will require additional expertise in the area of financial investigations. I would recommend using monies from the asset forfeiture funds in Treasury and Justice to help offset the cost.
- SOD needs to be designated as the Transnational Organized Crime (TOC) Coordination Center for the U.S.G. and should be provided the necessary enhancements, support and directives from the highest levels of government to support President Trump's Executive Orders on Transnational Crime and Violent Crime. The SOD Center currently has over

30 agencies represented to include the NYPD, UK, Canada and Australia and has years of operational multi-agency successes of fighting TOC. The DOD and Intelligence Community also have participation in the center so their equities are protected in the process.

- The DICE De-Confliction system, which is currently mandated by DOJ and DHS leadership, needs to be expanded to include the counter-terror investigations. The foundation has already been established. We also need the resources to ensure the DICE system is maintained, updated and refreshed.
- SOD has a robust International Investigations Program to go around the globe and take down huge threats working with our foreign counterparts around the globe. Since DEA has the largest worldwide presence of criminal investigators and years of experience working in the foreign arena, SOD, with input from all the agencies, is in a position to provide solid action plans on the highest level TOC targets.
- The leadership and command and control elements of the biggest threats to the United States are foreign and SOD has proven they can use the rule of law and obtain full cooperation from the counterparts to maximize the prosecutions in the United States.
- To illustrate the need for units such as CNTOC and added support from the new incoming leadership, one should read the December 19, 2016 article published by the Wall Street Journal titled, "The travels of Mrs. Murray's Toyota Unveils Terror-Finance Network". In this investigative article, the authors did a thorough job and reviewed the United States to Benin used car trade, which DEA and its partners had established, were involved in a global trade base money-laundering scheme to support Hezbollah's global operations. The WSJ concluded that the scheme is still operational and involved used- car businesses in the United States. The article goes on to describe the following disturbing facts: Many of the car dealers identified in the 311 initiative continued to ship cars to West Africa; the used-car export business to West Africa has expanded and is very active; the vehicle exports to Benin in 2015 totaled $434 million and were up from $47 million in 2005. (Christopher S. Stewart, 2016)
- Congress should earmark the required resources immediately to fund operations against TOC targets like Hezbollah and the Iran threat network and fully support the multi-agency task force approach described above.

References:

Center, P. (2009, July 09). Treasury Designates Medellin Drug Lord Tied to Oficina de Envigado Organized Crime G1roup. Retrieved from Treasury.gov: https://www.treasury.gov/press-center/press- releases/Pages/tg201.aspx

Center, P. (2011, February 10). Treasury Identifies Lebanese Canadian Bank Sal as a "Primary Money Laundering Concern" . Retrieved from Treasury.gov: https://www.treasury.gov/press-center/press-releases/Pages/tg1057.aspx

Center, P. (2011, January 26). Treasury Targets Major Lebanese-Based Drug Trafficking and Money Laundering Network . Retrieved from Treasury.gov: https://www.treasury.gov/press-center/press-releases/Pages/tg1035.aspx

Center, P. (2012, June 27). Treasury Targets Major Money Laundering Network Linked to Drug Trafficker Ayman Joumaa and a Key Hizballah Supporter in South America. Retrieved from Treasury.gov: https://www.treasury.gov/press-center/press-releases/Pages/tg1624.aspx

Christopher S. Stewart, R. B. (2016, December 19). The Travels of Mrs. Murray's Toyota Unveil Terror- Finance Network. Retrieved from wsj.com: http://www.wsj.com/articles/the-travels-of-mrs- murrays-toyota-unveils-terror-finance-network-1482163526

DEA. (2011, Dec 15). DEA News: Civil Suit Exposes Lebanese . Retrieved from DEA.gov:https://www.dea.gov/pubs/pressrel/pr121511.html

DEA. (2016, February 01). DEA and European Authorities Uncover Massive Hizballah Drug and Money Laundering Scheme. Retrieved from dea.gov: https://www.dea.gov/divisions/hq/2016/hq020116.shtml

EDVA. (2011, December 13). U.S. Charges Alleged Lebanese Drug Kingpin with Laundering Drug Proceeds for Mexican and Colombian Drug Cartels. Retrieved from Justice.gov: https://www.justice.gov/archive/usao/vae/news/2011/12/20111213joumaanr.html

Justice. (2012, August 20). Manhattan U.S. Attorney Announces Seizure Of $150 Million In Connection With A Hizballah-Related Money Laundering Scheme. Retrieved from Justice.gov: https://www.justice.gov/archive/usao/nys/pressreleases/August12/lcbseizure.html

Rotella, C. K. (2008, October 22). LA Times.com. Retrieved from Drug probe finds Hezbollah link: http://articles.latimes.com/2008/oct/22/world/fg-cocainering22

York, S. D. (2013, June 25). Manhattan U.S. Attorney Announces $102 Million Settlement Of Civil Forfeiture And Money Laundering Claims Against Lebanese Canadian Bank. Retrieved from Justice.gov: https://www.justice.gov/usao-sdy/pr/manhattan-us-attorney-announces-102-million-settlement-civil-forfeiture-and-money

Chairman ROYCE. Thank you, Mr. Maltz.
Mr. Szubin.

STATEMENT OF MR. ADAM SZUBIN, DISTINGUISHED PRACTITIONER-IN-RESIDENCE, JOHNS HOPKINS UNIVERSITY SCHOOL OF ADVANCED INTERNATIONAL STUDIES (FORMER ACTING UNDER SECRETARY FOR TERRORISM AND FINANCIAL INTELLIGENCE, U.S. DEPARTMENT OF THE TREASURY)

Mr. SZUBIN. Thank you, Chairman Royce, Ranking Member Engel, distinguished members of the committee. Thank you for convening the important hearing.

This committee has long been a strong advocate for the smart use of economic tools and for my former office at Treasury, the Office of Terrorism and Financial Intelligence. I want to thank you for that. And I want to particularly thank the chair and ranking member personally for their leadership and unfailing support.

If the policymaking community was too dismissive of sanctions 15 years ago, I am concerned that the pendulum has shifted and the tool is being used too readily now and in ways that risk undercutting its effectiveness. In my written testimony, I set out seven recommendations that I believe are key to preserving the power and influence of U.S. economic measures for decades to come, and I will outline them just very briefly here.

First, fund the effort. Even after some growth, the entire Treasury team that covers sanctions has fewer than 500 people, and that includes the intelligence, regulatory, licensing, targeting, compliance, enforcement, legal, and policy teams, administering every sanctions program from al-Qaeda to Zimbabwe. The staff are among the most dedicated you will find in government, but if we want them to continue to deliver highly professional and impactful results, Congress must equip them to succeed.

Two, strengthen our relationships abroad. Sanctions are not an alternative to diplomacy, they are an exercise of diplomacy. We need strong political leadership across the State Department, experienced career diplomats, and staffed Embassies, if we are to marshal the sanctions pressure we need in a globalized world.

Three, control sanctions policy. More than 30 U.S. States have passed sanctions laws that differ and depart from Federal law implicating Iran, Burma, Syria, Sudan. These States seek to alter the behavior of foreign governments but they are not subject to any congressional oversight. And State legislatures target not Iranian or Sudanese companies, but European and South Asian companies that are doing business in sanctioned countries—business, I would add, that is fully legal under their home laws and under U.S. Federal law.

I do not believe that individual States should be allowed to substitute their foreign policy judgment for that of Congress and the President. Congress should explicitly preempt the States in this field, or, at the very least, withhold its endorsement for State divestment and sanctions laws. Foreign policy is an area where we, as a country, must speak with one voice.

Four, enforce coherently. The success of sanctions, as we have heard today, depends on tough and rigorous enforcement. But we undermine our objectives when a constellation of local, State, and

Federal agencies simultaneously assert jurisdiction over sanctions violations and do not coordinate their activities.

There is no excuse for piling on with redundant penalties, and there is no reason for sanctions enforcement at any level to be occurring without the knowledge and input of OFAC, the agency that writes and interprets Federal sanctions.

Five, honor our word. It will be, as you all know, extraordinarily difficult to persuade North Korea to come to the negotiating table over its nuclear program. But we will have made a difficult challenge impossible if we are seen as a country that does not honor its promises when it comes to sanctions.

Regardless of one's view of the Iran nuclear deal, if we are perceived to be playing games with or discarding our sanctions commitments, while Iran is adhering to its commitments on the nuclear side, it would be foolish to expect North Korea to come to the table for a promise of U.S. sanctions relief.

I would note that when I say honoring our word, that does not mean taking the pressure off of Iran's malign activities outside of the nuclear sphere, to include the human rights violations we have witnessed so blatantly in recent weeks, their sponsorship of terrorism, notably Hezbollah, the IRGC, the Quds Force, and their missile program.

Six, ensure flexibility. Congress has enacted vitally important sanctions laws, helping the cause on Iran, on Sudan, on Russia. Historically, though, Congress recognized that statutory sanctions tend to be nearly impossible to repeal and provided waiver and licensing authorities so that the executive branch could deal with foreign threats as they evolved. This practice currently seems to be at risk.

Sanctions that cannot be eased without an affirmative joint resolution of Congress are a problem. They will be viewed by the target as written in stone and will be treated as a cost to be factored in rather than as an inducement to change behavior.

I urge Congress to adhere to its historical practice of providing waivers and licensing authority to the executive branch regardless of the sanctions context.

Finally, preserve our financial leverage. Russia and other adversaries have realized that the dominance of the West's financial system is a strategic liability when sanctions are imposed against them.

President Putin has pressed other countries to turn away from the West's banks and financial system and away from the dollar and the euro, but he has largely failed in this effort so far. Our institutions are known to be more capable, our markets more dependable, and our currency more attractive than any in the world.

To preserve this leverage, though, we must take care not to unintentionally drive governments and businesses away. As discussed, we have to be coordinated and clear in implementing sanctions so that foreign banks and businesses know that our system is tough but fair. We need to maintain our foreign relations and strive wherever possible to act in concert with others.

And, as tempting as it may be to tell the world that it can choose to do business in the U.S. dollar or with X country, we should be imposing secondary sanctions exceedingly rarely. If foreign actors come to see that the cost of doing business in the dollar is a whole-sale adoption of U.S. foreign policy, we will have lost leverage and done our adversaries' work for them.

To conclude, the U.S. enjoys many strategic advantages in the sanctions arena. If we preserve those strengths and act responsibly, I know that economic sanctions will help to advance our security and global security into the years and decades to come.

Thank you. I look forward to your questions.

[The prepared statement of Mr. Szubin follows:]

House Foreign Affairs Committee

"Sanctions and Financial Pressure: Major National Security Tools"

Testimony of Adam J. Szubin

Distinguished Practitioner-in-Residence

Johns Hopkins University, School of Advanced International Studies (SAIS)

January 10, 2018

Chairman Royce, Ranking Member Engel, and distinguished members of this committee, thank you for convening this important hearing and for inviting me to testify. More substantively, thank you for your longstanding bipartisan support to U.S. sanctions programs and to my former office, Treasury's Office of Terrorism and Financial Intelligence (TFI). This Committee has been a strong advocate for the smart use of economic statecraft and I hope that it will continue to use its leadership and influence to protect and preserve these tools for many years to come.

As someone who has worked in and studied the field of sanctions for the last 15 years, the developments are striking. One does not have to go back many years to remember a near consensus in the foreign affairs community that sanctions were ineffective and – worse – turned populations against us. I am hopeful that the binary question from that period – "Do sanctions work?" – is being replaced by more productive inquiries, such as "What threats/groups/nations are most susceptible to sanctions?", "What are the essential elements of an effective sanctions program?", and "How can we maximize our sanctions leverage and protect against countermeasures?".

In 2005, as the George W. Bush administration embarked on what was to be a years-long intensive sanctions campaign to address Iran's nuclear threat, we heard from some critics on the right that sanctions had been tried and failed, and that the only way to address Iran's nuclear program was through military force. Some on the left argued that sanctions would only drive the people of Iran into the arms of the ayatollahs. To your credit, Congress and the executive branch, under both Republican and Democratic leaders, saw things differently. Even those who were doubtful whether sanctions would ultimately yield results believed that we owed it to ourselves to put everything we had behind the effort given the urgency of the threat and the lack of good alternatives. And the U.S. Government did put everything it had behind the effort. President Bush and Secretary of State Rice directed Stuart Levey to draw up a multi-stage strategy and the Administration marshaled the intelligence, economic, and diplomatic resources necessary to drive it forward. In 2009, the Bush team handed it off to President Obama who sustained and built upon the effort. Congress, and this committee in particular, worked together in a bipartisan fashion, and passed tough and smart sanctions laws to intensify the impact of sanctions around the world. As the noose tightened, we saw the election of President Rouhani, and Iran finally came to the negotiating table to address the world's concerns about its then-burgeoning nuclear program. I remember the harrowing estimates in 2013 that Iran was 2-3 months from having enough enriched uranium for a nuclear bomb. It is now five years later, and Iran has not only not crossed that nuclear threshold, it has been pushed far away from it and has accepted an unprecedented nuclear inspection program.

The fact that the United States today confronts only one rogue nuclear state and not two is a testament to the steady work of Congress and two Administrations, and a credit to this Committee's support for tough and smart sanctions.

These days, sanctions have become the instrument of choice to confront vexing national security and foreign policy threats from human rights abuses to corruption, from terrorism to cybercrime. Both the executive and legislative branches have increasingly drawn on the tool and we have even witnessed dozens of U.S. state legislatures enacting their own sanctions laws. Indeed, if the policymaking community was too dismissive of sanctions fifteen years ago, I fear that the pendulum has swung too far in the other direction. I am concerned, honestly, that the tool is being used too readily and in ways that risk undercutting its effectiveness.

Nation states do not have many tools to influence hostile foreign countries and groups. We can turn to diplomacy, intelligence, military, or economic instruments when our interests and people are threatened from abroad. The largest and most daunting threats will not typically yield to diplomacy and intelligence. If we don't want to find ourselves deploying military force, we must preserve the strength of our economic and financial instruments. Unfortunately, while there are volumes written on the application of military force, we do not yet have a doctrine for the proper use of economic statecraft. This is not the place to set out such a doctrine. But I would respectfully offer seven practical and present-day recommendations that I believe are key if we want to preserve the power and influence of U.S. economic sanctions into the decades to come.

1. Fund the Effort

Sanctions have the odd distinction of being both the most popular and the least well-resourced tool of statecraft in our government. Even after some growth, the Treasury team that works on sanctions has fewer than 500 people. This includes the intelligence, regulatory, licensing, targeting, compliance, enforcement, legal, and policy teams, and they administer every sanctions program from al Qaida to Zimbabwe. Their responsibilities are growing far faster than their staffs. Moreover, many of these jobs require specialized skill sets and experience that take years to develop. The teams at Treasury are among the most dedicated I have seen in government, but if we want them to continue to deliver highly professional and impactful results, Congress must equip them to succeed.

2. Strengthen our Relationships

Sanctions are not an alternative to diplomacy, they are an exercise of diplomacy. In today's globalized economy, it is axiomatic that sanctions must be enforced multilaterally to succeed. That does not necessarily mean that a U.N. Security Council resolution is needed. Combined European and U.S. sanctions pressure after Russia invaded Ukraine imposed significant costs on Putin by depriving Russia of financing and technology that it could not obtain elsewhere. It does mean, however, that the U.S. cannot go it alone.

In every sanctions campaign in which I was involved, our success depended on support from foreign capitals, companies, and banks. We sought cooperation from financial centers, like London, Frankfurt, Tokyo, and Dubai; from multilateral institutions like the G-7; and from relevant regional institutions, like the Organization of American States, the Arab League, the Association of Southeast Asian Nations, or the African Union. Building that support requires concerted and serious diplomacy. In the realm of sanctions, the equation is fairly straightforward – if our foreign relationships deteriorate, we lose leverage. We need strong political leadership across the State Department, experienced career diplomats, and staffed embassies.

3. Control Sanctions Policy

Alongside the expansion in federal sanctions, there has been a proliferation of sanctions activity at the state level. More than thirty states have passed Iran-related sanctions laws that differ from federal law, and a rash of states have passed laws implicating Burma, Syria, and Sudan. These laws regulate state contracting, procurement, and investment and can have a meaningful impact on international commerce. Indeed, California's two largest pension funds together hold more assets than most of the world's central banks or sovereign wealth funds.

State sanctions laws have one purpose – to alter the behavior of foreign governments. And, because federal sanctions typically already restrict primary trade or investment with sanctioned countries, state legislatures typically impose pressure indirectly, by employing "secondary" or "extraterritorial" sanctions. These laws penalize not Iranian or Sudanese companies, but companies in the jurisdictions of our allies and partners that are, in turn, trading with or investing in sanctioned countries. Such secondary sanctions are highly controversial and diplomatically fraught; the companies targeted are behaving in ways that are legal in their countries and fully comply with U.S. sanctions laws. Should Massachusetts be allowed to substitute its judgment on foreign policy for that of Congress and the President? Do state legislators have the expertise and intelligence reporting at their disposal to do so wisely? How well do states monitor developments in foreign affairs and adapt their sanctions in response?

I believe that these sanctions, while politically popular, undermine the federal foreign policy prerogative. Congress should explicitly preempt the states in this field, and make clear that directing economic sanctions at foreign governments is an exclusively federal prerogative.

To the extent Congress is not willing to preempt the states actively, it should at the very least withdraw or withhold its endorsement of state divestment and sanctions laws. Foreign policy is an area where we must speak with one voice. As President Madison wrote in *Federalist Paper* No. 42, "[i]f we are to be one nation in any respect, it clearly ought to be in respect to other nations."

4. Enforce Coherently

If private actors do not fear consequences for evading sanctions, the measures are doomed to fail. The successes of U.S. sanctions, whether with respect to terrorist groups, narcotics cartels, or rogue regimes, have derived in no small part from the perception that the U.S. takes sanctions enforcement seriously. And we must absolutely continue to do so.

But we undermine our objectives when a constellation of local, state, and federal agencies simultaneously assert jurisdiction over sanctions enforcement and do not coordinate their activities. A financial institution can face sanctions enforcement from its federal banking supervisor, Treasury's Office of Foreign Assets Control, the Department of Justice, and – given the concentration of banking activity in New York – the New York State Department of Financial Services and the District Attorney of the County of New York. In the best of circumstances, all of the relevant agencies coordinate in advance and present a united enforcement approach. But this coordination is often lacking, which can result in inconsistent messages and outcomes in sanctions enforcement.

A few specific notes of concern. First, state and local enforcement authorities should not be interpreting sanctions requirements independent of federal authorities. There is no excuse for sanctions enforcement to be occurring at any level without the knowledge and input of OFAC, the agency charged with writing and interpreting the sanctions rules. In my past capacity as OFAC Director, I had to intervene to convince a state regulatory agency not to penalize transactions that OFAC had expressly authorized. If OFAC cannot authoritatively tell a private company what sanctions-related transactions are prohibited or allowed because a state or local enforcement agency may have different views, the strength of our national sanctions is at risk. And state and local agencies are not subject to congressional oversight. As the Supreme Court has noted, "[s]anctions are drawn not only to bar what they prohibit but to allow what they permit, and the inconsistency of sanctions here undermines the congressional calibration of force." Crosby v. National Foreign Trade Council, 530 U.S. 363, at 380 (2000). Unfortunately, we have experienced drift in this area in recent years.

Second, criminal authorities should prosecute companies and individuals who engage in willful misconduct. Negligence and compliance program weaknesses that are inevitable in large human enterprises should be handled by regulatory agencies.

Third, it is generally wasteful and detrimental for criminal prosecutors to require the hiring of private monitors in industries that are already highly regulated. A monitor may make eminent sense in a sector that is largely unsupervised, but the existing banking supervisory framework is more than adequate to the task of monitoring sanctions compliance, and I have yet to hear a convincing argument for a fourth of fifth "set of eyes" that would report to criminal prosecutors.

Fourth and finally, there is no sanctions advantage to piling on. Large sanctions violations warrant commensurately large penalties and willful violations may warrant prosecution. But having regulatory and enforcement agencies fine the identical conduct multiple times simply because they can does not advance sanctions objectives and undermines the perception of integrity. In my years at Treasury, our guiding principle was that a violating institution should pay a penalty that was serious and proportionate in the aggregate, not that it should pay such an amount multiple times because it had the misfortune to fall under the jurisdiction of multiple agencies.

5. Honor our Word

At best, it is extremely difficult to persuade a government to change a core policy by applying external economic pressure. In the case of Iran, it took eight years of pressure involving dozens of countries, four U.N. Security Council resolutions, multiple acts of Congress, and countless executive actions and designations to change Iran's calculus. Even those of us on the inside were never certain that it would work.

We now face odds that are arguably even more difficult with North Korea. But we will have made a difficult challenge impossible if we are seen as a country that does not honors its sanctions promises. Specifically, if we are perceived to be disregarding or playing games with our sanctions commitments while Iran is adhering to its nuclear commitments, it would be foolish to expect a North Korean government to make nuclear concessions in exchange for a promise of U.S. sanctions relief.

Conversely, we made no promises in the Iranian nuclear deal to withhold pressure against Iran's non-nuclear activities. It is appropriate and justified to target Iranian officials and networks responsible for human rights violations, cyberattacks, missile procurement, and terrorism.

6. Ensure Flexibility

Congress has a key role in the sanctions arena, as I saw firsthand. From Iran to Sudan to Russia, Congress enacted powerful authorities to protect our financial system and to pressure foreign threats. That said, statutory sanctions work differently from executive branch sanctions – they tend to be broader, more blunt, and almost impossible to repeal. If we want foreign governments to sit down with our Secretary of State and negotiate an end to hostile behavior, we must give the executive branch the discretion to lighten or remove the pressure. If the sanctions target perceives sanctions to be written in stone, those sanctions have ceased to act as a motivator for change and exist solely as a penalty, whose costs will be factored in.

Historically, where Congress has codified sanctions into law, it has preserved the necessary flexibility. Like guardrails on a highway, codification laws ensured that the executive branch would continue driving in the right direction but allowed it to adjust its speed and lane in response to diplomatic developments. The Jackson-Vanik Amendment provides a good case study. Congress passed the law in 1974 to pressure the Soviet Union and its allies to ease restrictions on "refuseniks," including Soviet Jews who had been barred from practicing their religion or emigrating. When the Supreme Soviet passed a law codifying the end of emigration restrictions in 1991, President George H. W. Bush invoked the waiver provisions in the Jackson-Vanik Amendment and ended those sanctions on the Soviet Union. The waiver provisions in Jackson-Vanik were meaningful but workable, allowing the President to waive sanctions if the waiver would substantially promote the objectives of the law. If Congress disagreed, it could overrule the president's use of the waiver through a joint resolution. (Notably, Congress did not repeal the Jackson-Vanik Amendment until late 2012, a decade after the Soviet Union fell.)

In my view, the Jackson-Vanik Amendment took the right approach to codification. It imposed guardrails on the executive branch, but not a straitjacket. Sanctions that cannot be eased without an affirmative joint resolution of Congress are not likely to incentivize behavioral change from their target. Likewise, it is counter-productive to codify sanctions in a way that only allows for easing once the ultimate objectives of the sanctions have been obtained. Those that conduct our nation's foreign affairs must retain discretion to recognize and reward substantial progress or we may not see that progress arrive.

7. Preserve our Financial Leverage

Finally, we have to preserve the primacy of our financial system, which gives our sanctions such formidable strength. Russia and China are by now both aware of and resentful of their reliance on the West's financial system for financing, international payments, and investment. Russia is especially set on addressing this strategic vulnerability, and we see Putin mandating Russian alternatives to U.S. financial institutions and the U.S. dollar wherever he can. When it comes to business with third countries, though, Russia has not found a widespread willingness to abandon the dollar and the West. Our institutions are seen as more accountable, our infrastructure as more resilient, and our currency as the safest and most attractive in the world.

We can be assured, however, that Russia and our other adversaries will continually be pressing other countries to move away from the West's financial infrastructure, and away from the dollar and the euro. We cannot make their work easier for them. New payment methods and virtual currencies should be subjected to the same transparency and reporting requirements as traditional methodologies. And, as discussed above, we need to be smart, coherent, and coordinated in imposing and enforcing sanctions, so foreign businesses know that our markets and regulatory system are predictable and fair. As tempting as it may be to impose secondary sanctions and tell the world that it can choose to do business in the U.S. dollar or with X country, we should do so exceedingly rarely. If foreign actors come to perceive that the cost of doing business in the U.S. and in the dollar is wholesale adoption of U.S. foreign policy, we will have eroded our sanctions leverage and done our adversaries' work for them.

Conclusion

The United States enjoys many advantages in the field of economic sanctions. We have tremendous leverage stemming from our economic strength, our close partnerships with other economic leaders, and the primacy of the U.S. dollar and U.S. financial institutions. We have also grown more experienced and smarter in our use of economic tools. If we preserve these assets, I believe that economic sanctions can protect and advance American and global security into the years and decades to come.

Chairman ROYCE. Thank you, Adam.

I will go now to the ranking member, Mr. Engel, for his opening remarks.

Mr. ENGEL. Thank you, Mr. Chairman. And thank you, once again, for calling this very important hearing.

I have to say we are kicking off the committee's work for 2018 on a somber note, Mr. Chairman. As we all know by now, this will be your last year in the House. You and I took our respective positions on this committee at the same time, 5 years ago, and since then you have run this committee in a way that makes us the most bipartisan committee in Congress.

I know you know that I have deeply valued our partnership and our friendship, and I am proud of the work that we have done together, and I look forward to our final year of working together. So thank you, Mr. Chairman.

Chairman ROYCE. Thank you, Mr. Engel. I appreciate it.

Mr. ENGEL. To our witnesses, welcome back to the Foreign Affairs Committee. We are grateful for your time and eager to hear your views on how we can make sanctions more effective.

Mr. Maltz, tell me you are from New York.

Mr. MALTZ. I am from Mobile, Alabama, sir. Just a joke.

Mr. ENGEL. Well, I am from the Bronx, so I can pick up that accent any time with my eyes closed.

Mr. MALTZ. Are you a Yankee fan?

Mr. ENGEL. Well, I root for both of them. I will give you a politician's answer. I like the Mets too.

I consider sanctions to be an important tool for dealing with problematic actors on the global stage. We know that if we use them well, sanctions can help change harmful behavior. This committee, under the chairman's leadership, has passed numerous sanctions bills and we have worked with successive administrations to see these measures put in place all over the world. And these are the areas I would like to focus on today.

First, there is North Korea. The root of this challenge, of course, is the Kim regime's nuclear ambitions. Congress has done its part to deal with this challenge, thanks largely to the leadership of Chairman Royce, by ratcheting up sanctions again and again on Pyongyang and the regime's supporters.

I remember being in North Korea many years ago as a North Korean high government official said to us: Saddam Hussein didn't have nuclear weapons, and look where he is now. So it was clear, even way back then, that they regarded nuclear weapons as their chip, and nothing has really changed.

But as the danger escalates, we are seeing that U.S. sanctions are only one piece of the puzzle. China is key to enforcement. But China is prone to cheating. And at the same time, the United States has been reluctant to sanction big Chinese financial institutions. And even if there were universal enforcement of sanctions around the world, there is little to believe sanctions alone, particularly in the short-term, would push Kim to give up his nuclear weapons.

So, in the case of North Korea, I think diplomacy is a key complement to a sanctions package. And here, I fear, the administration is making things worse. The President's comments on North

Korea have been inflammatory, most recently with the President's button-measuring contest over Twitter. These actions increase the risk of miscalculation. And when we are talking about nuclear weapons on the Korean Peninsula, or anywhere else, there is absolutely no margin for error.

As Mr. Szubin points out in his testimony, we need smart, reasoned diplomacy to go hand-in-hand with our sanctions. And if we don't have that, if we don't have a diplomatic strategy, aren't we just raising tensions and raising the risk of a military conflict?

Secondly is Iran. This committee, again under the chairman's leadership, has done more with Iran than I think all other committees combined. Here is an example when sanctions were essential for bringing Iranians to the negotiating table.

Now, I wasn't pleased with the outcome. The Iran nuclear agreement, everyone here knows I voted against it. But there is no doubt that without international sanctions these talks would never have gone forward.

And, even though I disagreed with the nuclear deal, I think we need to keep up our end of the bargain. That means we should shy away from sanctions that would cause the United States to violate the terms of the agreement. This is no longer 2015, it is 2017, and I think we ought to keep the agreement and enforce it.

However, we should use every tool at our disposal to go after Iran's other harmful activities: Support for terrorism, ballistic missile development, human rights abuses. Again, this committee has passed numerous sanctions bills targeting the regime and its supporters. We want to see these sanctions fully implemented, and we should keep looking for ways to tighten the screws even more.

And, lastly, Russia. We have imposed—again, this committee has been at the helm—we have imposed a range of sanctions against Russia, responding to the seizure of Crimea, to the ongoing conflict in eastern Ukraine, to the serial abuse of human rights by the Putin government.

Yesterday, our Ambassador to Russia, Jon Huntsman, met with our members on the Foreign Affairs Committee and he telegraphed a potential shift in policy, which I interpreted as possibly scaling back sanctions to incentivize Putin to change his behavior.

I don't agree with that. I think that is a misguided approach. I think we need to go back to the well again and again to let Putin know he is leading his country into isolation. And that path must include sanctions dealing with Russia's attack on American democracy.

A year has gone by since our intelligence agencies gave us the details about Russian meddling in the 2016 election. This administration has held no one accountable, and that is just baffling.

We are now, once again, in an election year and by the administration's own admission, Russia is going to use that playbook once again. CIA Director Pompeo said so. Ambassador Huntsman said so.

We passed new sanctions on Russia last year to deal with this. This committee was essential in passing those new sanctions, so it is law, but the administration has yet to use them. How can we possibly hope to deter this sort of behavior if we leave our best tools sitting on the shelf?

Maybe we need tougher measures that would force the administration to act, like the bill I introduced with Mr. Connolly, the SECURE Our Democracy Act. One way or the other, we need to do something because right now the door is wide open to another attack on our democracy, and that should trouble all of us.

So I hope our witnesses will shed additional light on these issues. We have heard their opening statements and look forward to your answering our questions.

I thank the chairman, and I yield back.

Chairman ROYCE. Thank you, Mr. Engel.

I would like to start with Mr. Zarate, a statement you made, and Mr. Szubin.

Mr. Zarate, you testified that over the past 15 years sanctions have become the tools of first resort and even our central strategies in dealing with the hardest national security challenges we face.

And Mr. Szubin, you characterized sanctions as having the odd distinction of being both the most popular and least well-resourced tool of statecraft in our Government. And you raised the concern about not having enough resources to carry out sanctions.

So do Treasury and other agencies involved in implementing sanctions have the manpower and other resources, like modern IT infrastructure, that they need to fully enforce the sanctions bill that this committee has championed?

Mr. Zarate, if you would like to start.

Mr. ZARATE. Mr. Chairman, I think Adam and I are coincident in the conclusion that these strategies and tools fit within that gap between diplomacy and kinetic action and then enable all the other things that matter in terms of our national security, our intelligence gathering, our law enforcement, our diplomacy, et cetera, and our military action.

I think a key challenge here is we are now at a point where we are potentially depending too much on these tools, assuming they will be a silver bullet to respond to every aggravation or problem. And I see this in three ways.

One is I think there is a lack of creativity as to how you then use financial measures in concert with other tools. And I think that has played out over time in the context of North Korea. It has played out to a certain extent with Iran, although I think our Iran campaign was one of the most sophisticated the U.S. Government has ever deployed. It is playing out in the context of Russia where response to Russian aggression be it in the virtual world or in the physical world can be both in the virtual and physical world and can include financial measures. So I think there is a lack of creativity as to how you deploy them.

Your question on the resources is an important one because I think we are underresourced in three ways. One is—I agree with Adam—we don't have enough people or resources at Treasury. This is the war room for how we deploy these strategies which are now essential to our national security. Let's resource it in a way that is appropriate.

Two, we don't have the information-sharing and technology infrastructure to allow the government now to aggregate data, to use predictive analytics, to begin to use artificial intelligence, to understand where there are systemic vulnerabilities and ties between the networks that matter to our national security.

And, third, we are not putting enough energy and resources, to Derek's point, into bringing together task forces that bring Federal agencies, as well as State and local agencies, that then get you to the consistency of approach and enforcement that we want, and, frankly, the urgency around North Korea, Iran, Russia, et cetera. Why we don't have task forces up and running on all of these issues, using the full weight and force of our authorities, is beyond me. I know there is a ton of work happening. I don't want to sug- gest that that is not happening. But there needs to be an all-out effort if we are to try a maximalist approach, for example, with North Korea, to avoid war and to try to change behavior.

Chairman ROYCE. And I will go to Mr. Szubin so you can raise again your concerns about having sufficient resources to carry out sanctions given your experience in that position.

Mr. SZUBIN. Mr. Chairman, I agree with you wholeheartedly. I think the effort needs more resources.

And when I would sit around the National Security Council table, if there was a tasking that went back on the defense side, had this massive apparatus. The same with intelligence, the same with diplomacy, although to a lesser extent. And then there was Treasury and we were sort of the little brother at the table, but over the years keep being asked to do more and more, sometimes by Congress, sometimes by the executive branch.

And these days it is really tough to think about a national security or foreign policy threat where we are not using sanctions and where we are not——

Chairman ROYCE. But you were partly—you are partly a victim of the successes. I mean, when we captured Viktor Bout, when we were successful in terms of bringing pressure on Iran, when we found we were having impact in slowing the race to weaponry in North Korea, all of this created this incentive to double down with the one thing that was working in order to really stretch the ability of these regimes to have access to the resources they wanted to carry out terror. And that was what you do.

And I don't think there is a sufficient comprehension in the other agencies of government in terms of the linchpin here. And that is one of the things I would like to drive through this hearing today. And I appreciate, again, your all calling attention to this.

I am out of time. I am going to go to Mr. Engel for his questions.

Mr. ENGEL. Thank you.

I want to raise something that I raised in my opening statement and something that we have talked about a great deal in this com- mittee since we were really responsible for the legislation. So let me throw this out to any of the witnesses who would care to an- swer.

Has the U.S. sanctioned anyone in Russia for the election inter- ference that CIA Director Pompeo said is ongoing? And, if not, do any of our witnesses know why not?

And do you think this inaction, this total failure to hold Russia accountable, has contributed to Russia's ongoing efforts to interfere with our democracy again, as CIA Director Pompeo recently said.

And, finally, do you think sanctions would be an effective way to punish those who carry out this attack and deter future operations along these lines?

Anyone who would care to answer that.

Mr. SZUBIN. I am happy to start, Congressman.

Toward the end of my time, toward the end of the Obama administration, we did, indeed, issue sanctions against a number of Russian entities who we believed, and who were, responsible for interference in the 2016 election. That included their intelligence agencies and some of the related fields and companies who were enabling them from a cyber perspective.

The bottom line, though, I think, of your question is, have we done enough? And to that, I agree, we have not. Neither this administration nor the prior administration have done enough to ensure that we will be safer in next year's coming elections, or in elections in 3 years, from Russian interference.

And I think this has to be much bigger than just sanctions. Yes, we should continue to put economic pressure on Russia. But as Juan was saying earlier, it has to be a whole-of-government approach, both in defending our electoral systems against cyber attacks and in making clear to Russia and other would-be interfering countries, this is unacceptable.

Elections are at the core of our country, and if the American people lose faith, lose trust in the integrity of those elections, I, frankly, fear for what that does to our country. We have to make a strong stand.

Mr. ENGEL. Thank you. Especially since this Congress passed the authority of the President to impose new sanctions, and they are just waiting there, they haven't been done.

Anybody else? Mr. Zarate?

Mr. ZARATE. Ranking Member Engel, I would like to address a couple of your points.

I am a firm believer that sanctions can be incredibly effective in the cyber domain to deter actors who are willing to use malicious cyber activity to affect U.S. interests.

This is a field, though, that grows more complicated as we have to then demonstrate with evidence and proof both in the context of the application of sanctions and then the public disclosure the attribution of the attacks.

And so, though I am a firm believer that we should be using sanctions targeted to dissuade and deter actors from affecting our democratic systems or trying to attack our systems, whether it is Russia, North Korea, Iran, all of which have done that very same thing, it has to be recognized that this is a more difficult task and often one filled with more sensitivities for the intelligence community.

So I just want to mention that there is great promise in their use but also great complication.

Another point is I think it is critical that we think about the use of other sanctions programs to deter the Russians or any other actor that is trying to affect U.S. interests. This administration has designated Russian actors under other sanctions programs. For example, in aid of North Korea there have been Russian entities designated. So I think that is an important dimension as well.

And then the physical dimension is critical too. The fact that we have made now a decision, the administration has made a decision to send anti-tank weaponry to Kiev is actually an incredibly important signal and a deterrent to Russia that we are taking very seriously not just what they are doing in Ukraine, but also what they are doing to affect U.S. interests.

And so I think this has to be viewed holistically, in part because the Russians, the Chinese, and others don't view this just in a cyber domain or in a physical domain or in the context of particular silos, but as a whole approach for their national security.

Mr. ENGEL. Thank you.

Mr. Szubin, let me ask you this about Iran. To what extent do you believe that sanctions have been effective, since the announcement of the JCPOA, in changing Iran's calculus vis-a-vis Iran's non-nuclear destabilizing activities? Is there room for improvement in our sanctions regime?

Mr. SZUBIN. There is always room to do more, and I am confident that my former colleagues at Treasury and across the administration are working very hard at identifying additional strategies and targets, whether on the ballistic missile side, on the support for terrorism, human rights, and on and on.

To what extent has the JCPOA framework been effective, been successful? I think it has done what it was designed to do, which is we had a nuclear deal, we had commitments on the nuclear side, and in exchange we lifted nuclear sanctions only, keeping a very robust set of measures, U.S. sanctions that prohibit almost all dealings between Iran and the United States and secondary sanctions that still in place today for any foreign company or bank that does business with the IRGC, with the Quds Force, with a ballistic missile company.

These sanctions have kept the pressure on Iran's other activities, and in some ways you can look at the protests that have gone on in recent weeks in Iran as being a reflection where the Iranian people say, wait a minute, we didn't get full sanctions relief, we were promised an economic turnaround and it didn't come.

And Iran has its own leadership to blame when it comes to why that opening didn't come. The leaders were not ready to make commitments to bring themselves into compliance with international expectations on terrorism, on ballistic missile. On the more technical levels, they were not ready to introduce transparency and financial sector reforms so that foreign investors could know who they are actually doing business with when they touch down in Tehran.

In all of these levels, I think the Iranian leadership has disappointed its own people, and you see that frustration coming out now. Our sanctions are a continued reflection of where Iran continues to not do what it needs to do.

Mr. ENGEL. Thank you.

Thank you, Mr. Chairman.

Chairman ROYCE. Thank you.

We will go to Ileana Ros-Lehtinen.

Ms. ROS-LEHTINEN. Thank you so much, Chairman Royce. And I echo the ranking member's words of praise about your bipartisan leadership in this committee, Mr. Chairman, and you will be missed. We want to see your portrait up here. Thank you so much. And this is an important and timely hearing because this an issue that Ranking Member Engel, Chairman Royce, I, and so many of our colleagues on this committee have been working on for quite some time, sanctions. I have authored sanctions bills that have become laws, including some of the strongest sanctions, like the Iran, North Korea, and Syria Nonproliferation Act and the Iran Threat Reduction and Syria Human Rights Act.

And I have been doing that working with the chairman and ranking member. And, also, we have authored others that aim to help people around the world in their fight for freedom and democracy, such as the Venezuela Human Rights and Democracy Protection Act.

And what is universally true for all of our sanctions law is that for sanctions to be truly effective, they have got to be fully implemented, vigorously enforced. And over the past 20 years Congress has given administration after administration all the tools necessary to help achieve some of our foreign policy objectives.

Unfortunately, not every administration has used these tools in order to maximize the impact of the sanctions. And most egregious was the Obama administration's fundamental misunderstanding of our Iran sanctions. The intent was not simply to bring Iran to the table. It was for Iran to abandon completely its nuclear weapons ambitions, to stop all of the enrichment, and to dismantle the nuclear program.

And the result of this misunderstanding is what we see this week as this administration must make certain certifications and decisions on Iran sanctions because of this weak and dangerous nuclear deal. And many of the discussions, both leading up to and following the nuclear deal, have centered around how Congress can ensure that administrations are not able to ignore or evade a congressional intent.

So with respect to our Iran sanctions or, like, INKSNA, or more generally, we need to find a way to close the loopholes or reconcile congressional intent with administrative implementation. And I hope this hearing gets us to where we want to be.

But, Mr. Maltz, I wanted to ask you, there was a report last month alleging the previous administration impeded or at least did not pursue some efforts to go after Hezbollah activities. It was a big news item. It was abundantly clear that the administration's Iran policy was driven strictly by its pursuit of a nuclear deal with Iran. And then, once secured, what it wanted to do was to preserve it.

But your testimony focuses on Project Cassandra and how we can improve going forward. Iran and Hezbollah's presence in the Western Hemisphere is pervasive and threatening. How can we improve the capabilities and cooperation of the governments of the region in making sure that they can stem this problem?

Mr. MALTZ. So thank you for the question. I mean, I know firsthand your level of engagement because when I was the head of SOD I frequently met with you and your people to discuss folks like Walid Makled and General Carvajal that were let go to go back to their country of Venezuela when you know, probably better than I, the connectivity to the military intelligence and the corruption and the weapons and the FARC. And also, as you know from studying this for years, they also had the connectivity of global drug trafficking around the world to generate funds.

So, number one, let's talk about the resources. You need the right resources. Let's stop wasting government taxpayers' money by creating redundancies. People don't even know what we already have, like the centers like the Special Operations Division.

I am not waving the flag for them, but I lived it for 10 years. There are centers that actually do have some good foundation that we need to build on. We don't need to create new centers and waste money.

For an example, to answer your question, we have the Australians, the Canadians, the Brits, who are all inundated with cocaine, for an example. Do you know that in Australia they are selling, still, cocaine, almost $250,000 a kilogram? And people wonder why terrorist organizations are moving cocaine. If you sell cocaine in America, it is like $35,000 I guess, $40,000. I am a little bit rusty on my updates. But I know for sure in Australia it is still up like $240,000. At one point, it was 300.

So you have to bring these countries together too. Europol, they are doing tremendous work over in Europe to bring people together, to bring intelligence together. But we need sound prosecution. Go after them right here. Because they don't want to come back to America. And we have tremendous capabilities to get them, and we have tremendous laws. We have some really good prosecutors that are still out there that will help us.

So if you get them back and you use, like—I don't want to pump up Adam, but OFAC and FinCEN, for an example. They are the ones that educated me on these powerful 981(k)'s, the 311 actions. You have to put that on steroids, and you have to have somebody accountable. If you are not willing to designate somebody to be responsible to the taxpayer to pull this together, it is never going to work.

Ms. ROS-LEHTINEN. Thank you so much.

Thank you, Mr. Chairman, Ranking Member.

Chairman ROYCE. Mr. Brad Sherman.

Mr. SHERMAN. I think we all want to associate ourselves with the remarks of the ranking member about our chairman. You will be missed, and we look forward to working with you for this year.

Sanctions are derided because they are hostile. But those who prize peace should be informed that they are not a prelude to war but a substitute for it. They do indeed often harm the innocent, particularly the U.S. companies that can't do business and jobs cannot be created. But the blame for that must be on the rogue regimes that necessitate sanctions, not on those who propose them. Sanctions have worked. In fact, they have worked better over the last 50 years than major military interventions. We look to South Africa, and we look to Iran, where the only argument, a fierce argument, was whether sanctions got us a good deal or more sanctions would have gotten us a better deal. No one argued that we should have not had sanctions and allowed the Iranians to move forward unimpeded.

Sanctions can work only if they are multinational. There is plenty of business to be done in Europe and Asia. We have to get their buy-in. And that can be done only through a combination of pressure and persuasion.

As to persuasion, we need a robust State Department. It is being cut back. That is a national security issue.

And, second, as we try to get the world to go along with us on issues important to our national security, all of our efforts in the world sphere should be designed to win friends and influence people. And even when we can't or choose not to go along with international consensus, doing so in a polite manner might be better than attacking, verbally and unnecessarily, most actors in the world.

But you also need pressure. You look at the Iran sanctions. They cut off Iran from European and Asian banks. They did so because we persuaded Europe and Asia that we have legitimate concerns, and we pressured their banks with possible denial of access to the U.S. banking system. If either of those elements hadn't been there, it would not have been effective.

And, finally, we have to have realistic objectives. We would not have gotten European and Asian support if we were demanding sanctions until there was regime change in Iran. Likewise, as we try to sanction North Korea, we will not have the support of China if they think that our objective is regime change. And, in addition, the regime itself is not going to reach a compromise with us due to sanctions if our objective is regime change.

Mr. Maltz, I do partially disagree with you. You talk about the importance of sharing information. But we went too far when, then, Bradley Manning had access to everything. And I think we need to have the balance between sharing information among those involved in law enforcement and intelligence and guarding information. We went too far in one direction. Now we maybe go—certainly, if you have a private with access to everything, you have gone too far to the other.

Many who have involved themselves in foreign policy their whole lives tend to support maximum executive branch power. Most have spent most of their time dealing with the executive branch. But Article I appears in our Constitution before Article II. And I think Mr. Szubin was arguing that our sanctions laws should give the maximum possible discretion to the executive branch. Perhaps I have that wrong. But if you didn't say that, somebody said it at some point, and I disagree with whoever that was.

But one thing I noted was your belief that we should honor our word. And I will agree with you except, who is the "our"? If we decide that any President can bind the American people permanently for anything they agree to, whether Congress votes in favor of it or not, even with a simple majority in both houses, then I think we have simply skipped Article I of the Constitution.

And while I support continuing the Iran deal—which, of course, was not approved by Congress—that does not mean that I am going to support saying that the American people have given their solemn word and are bound forever by anything this President chooses to agree to with Putin or anyone else.

So I hope that we would educate all of our international partners that we have a Constitution. They are welcome to read it. We will give them free copies. Call my office. We have got copies there. And that it provides, in effect, for both treaties and for legislative executive agreements, but it does not provide that the American people are bound because a President gives our word, a President gives his or her word. And if they want to give the word of the American people, they need to come to the United States Congress.

And I have exceeded my time.

Ms. ROS-LEHTINEN [presiding]. Thank you, Mr. Sherman. Thank you very much.

Mr. Rohrabacher of California.

Mr. ROHRABACHER. Thank you very much.

And I appreciate your testimony today. It has been very thought provoking.

Let me just note that we have the Magnitsky Act in place. Now, I didn't support naming it the Magnitsky Act, but I supported the act itself. And, with that, we now have the ability to single out individuals who are participating in human rights abuses in other countries, something I have long supported. And we now, thus, have the ability to take members of the Revolutionary Guard in Iran and making them what they are, criminals, and put them on the list of international criminals.

I take it that you support that?

Mr. ZARATE. Yes.

Mr. ROHRABACHER. All right.

Let me note that Iran, in terms of what comments we have had about the President and the Iranian arms deal, let me just note that the President of the United States, as part of the Iran deal, has been tasked with verifying compliance with that deal, okay?

All our position should be is this President should tell the truth, whatever it is. If they are in compliance, they are in compliance, and if they are not, they are not. And we shouldn't be trying to just push the President in one direction or the other or claim that he is playing politics when he has been given that responsibility. So that is number two.

But what I would really like to go into—and I am sorry for your brother's loss in Afghanistan. I have spent a lot of time and effort on Afghan issues, as people know.

One of the things that has disturbed me during all of these years, we have a long time ago could have eliminated the poppy crops, the opium production in Afghanistan. We could have done that easily years ago. And I have been involved with some classified approaches to that and it would have been easy to do. We have not.

Your brother and other people's sons and brothers from the United States have lost their lives because we have not cut off the funding, as we could have long ago, to opium production. And it seems to me that indicates that there are powerful economic forces at play preventing us from doing what is right by those who are going over there to defend us.

Maybe you have some thoughts on that.

Mr. MALTZ. Well, the first thought is going back to Mr. Sherman's comment, because it has to be clarified. Everything we did at the Special Operations Division was pursuant to the rule of law. So we are 100 percent in support of the Constitution and to bring these people to justice in the greatest country of the world.

We don't believe in information sharing to people that shouldn't have access to the information. But if you have a government task force set up to go after the threats to this country, we need to share information. You can't have a system where our terrorist investigators don't share with the criminal investigators. That is a recipe for disaster.

And, by the way, 16 years after 9/11, what we did and what we implemented with information sharing is exactly what the American public would expect. There is no politics in information sharing.

Mr. ROHRABACHER. I have only got a minute and a half.

Mr. MALTZ. I am sorry, sir, but I had to address that, because that really was irritating.

Mr. ROHRABACHER. I wish you would have done in Brad's time, however, but that is okay, because we don't share information here.

Mr. MALTZ. But as far as Afghanistan, I am not an expert on eradicating the poppies. I am not saying I disagree or agree. We are on the operation side. We saw the nexus between the Taliban and the drug traffickers.

Mr. ROHRABACHER. Okay. Let me just note this. It is not just the poppies. What we have got is we know someone is financing ISIL, someone is financing these terrorists. There are huge financial interests to these international financial institutions that obviously are involved and we have let them go. We have not focused on them.

Mr. MALTZ. I agree.

Mr. ROHRABACHER. It is called blood money, especially when people like yourself and others have lost relatives and friends and sons and daughters to this terrorism.

I would suggest we need to focus on the international financial institutions that are engaged in this, spend the same type of effort as we have talked about with the Magnitsky Act of focusing on those specific individuals that are engaged in this type of behavior that is financing terrorism.

And the money is going somewhere, the crooked banks—or, excuse me, the crooked leaders from Third World countries that are being bought off by the Chinese to steal the minerals from those countries. It is disgraceful. We are letting that go. I have yet to see major banks having someone sent to jail for being an accomplice to terrorism and ripping off Third World countries.

So anyway, with that said, thank you for your testimony today.

Thank you, Ed, for your leadership on this and many others issues.

Chairman ROYCE [presiding]. Thank you, Dana. Thank you.

We now go to Mr. Gregory Meeks from New York.

Mr. MEEKS. Thank you, Mr. Chairman. I want to join the ranking member in saying it has been an honor serving on this committee with you. And you will surely be missed not being here with us after this term. Look forward to the best.

So let me just first say that I was sitting here stretching my imagination trying to see or remember a unilateral sanctions deal that was successful. And I can't think of one where the Congress or anyone in the United States—we are the greatest country—where we do something unilaterally and it is successful.

Any time sanctions have worked, it has been in conjunction in a multilateral agreement with other countries. That is how you put pressure on. So as big the military we have and everything else, it is working with other countries to figure out how we sanction someone to make them come to not just the United States' will, but the world's population.

That is tremendously important. It is in my estimation the only reason why we have a sanctions bill that is working and is successful in Iran. So I am concerned about what may or may not take place next week.

So I will go to Mr. Szubin first, because the administration is expected to decide whether or not to follow the agreements under the Iran nuclear deal and U.S. relevant sanctions on Iran.

Now, I know that if we exit, our European allies will not, I have talked to them, I know that China and Russia will not, we have talked to them. And I am concerned that if the Trump administration decides that, despite the fact that the nuclear deal is working, it will impose sanctions anyway, and then the message to the world will be that America cannot be trusted to uphold the deal.

So, Mr. Szubin, what do you see as the potential consequences if Iran sanctions are not waived in accordance with the Iran agreement, whether or not our allies will see this as a breach of the agreement and a breach of trust, and sanctions in Iran at this time would give hardliners.

So my concern is, I want to help the moderates. I don't want to help the hardliners. But what message? Would this help the hardliners in Iran and hurt the current protesters in Iran because we have got to do this and lose the leverage, if you will, with Iran if the administration decides to waive sanctions?

Mr. SZUBIN. Thank you, Congressman. And I very much agree with your objective and your outlook on the situation. I wrote an op-ed a couple of weeks ago called "Don't Let Iran Out of the Box," and it was addressing exactly this point.

Iran's leaders today find themselves in a box. On the nuclear side, they are hemmed in. Instead of being 2 to 3 months away from enough enriched uranium for a nuclear weapon they are more than a year away, reversing where they had been in 2011, 2012, 2013, and that will be the case for the foreseeable you future.

The inspectors are crawling over Iran and we have better data than we ever had about Iran's program and we don't have any information from any observer that Iran is in material breach of its commitments.

Why would we let them out of that box? We have to let those nuclear constraints keep Iran subject to those nuclear constraints, on the one hand.

On the economic side, this windfall that many predicted has not come to Iran. There never were $100 billion, $150 billion in assets. That is a make believe number. Iran's true benefit from the deal was significant, but it was nowhere near enough to get them out of the hole that they were in—a hole, by the way, that they dug for themselves. And that is what you see now playing out with the economic frustration in the streets of Tehran and in other cities across Iran.

So Iran's rule letters are not riding high because of the nuclear deal. The nuclear deal is constraining their program and their economy is constrained. If we walk away from this deal, we are letting them out, maybe out of one, maybe out of both of those two boxes, and I think it would be very foolish and self-defeating for us as a country.

Mr. MEEKS. And hurting our leverage also.

Mr. SZUBIN. Absolutely.

Mr. MEEKS. So the other—and I only have 29 seconds so—but the other issue that I am concerned with is the lack of funding of our State Department and the reshaping of Foggy Bottom. In particular, the position of sanctions coordinator was eliminated, and that was the person that would coordinate with our multilateral partners.

And so not having that person in place so that we could make sure that sanctions are being applied in an appropriate way, particularly as we talk about the sanctions on Russia, does that not then give us a problem to ensure the enforcement of those multilateral sanctions on Russia are lived up to?

Mr. SZUBIN. So on this point, I would say, Congressman, I worked in the field of sanctions and government for about 15 years, and State has had different formulations in terms of who it asked, what office it asked to coordinate sanctions. Sometimes it asked its North Korea or its Iran office, sometimes there was a special envoy.

The idea of an Ambassador to head up that function at State was relatively recent and it doesn't trouble me whether that position is done away with. What is important, in my view, is that there be somebody at a high level who is charged with seeing that mission through. Right now there is a very good official at the State Department who used to work with us at Treasury who is running that function at State, and I think it is in good hands.

But to your broader point, yes, the State Department needs to be staffed, the political positions need to be filled, because sanctions don't work without a concerted global effort, and it is our Ambassadors who carry that message forward.

Chairman ROYCE. Mr. Steve Chabot of Ohio.

Mr. CHABOT. Thank you, Mr. Chairman. And thank you for holding this important hearing.

First, I would like to request that a recent Politico op-ed, titled, "The List That is Freaking Out Everyone in Moscow," be included in the record.

Chairman ROYCE. Without objection.

Mr. CHABOT. Thank you.

This op-ed discusses section 241 of the Countering America's Adversaries Through Sanctions Act, CAATSA, a bill that you, Mr. Chairman, introduced in our committee and President Trump signed into law last August.

Section 241 requires the Secretary of the Treasury to issue a report identifying the most significant senior foreign political figures and oligarchs in the Russian Federation as determined by their closeness to the Russian regime and their net worth.

Being named to the report could result in U.S. sanctions. The threat of being cut off from the banking system and network could have a significant impact on its own; however, even without sanctions being put on the list, would at the very least make it more difficult to do business with the West and the U.S. in particular. So it is my hope that the administration gives serious consideration to section 241 of CAATSA.

Before I get to a question on that, let me add something separate.

Mr. Szubin, while we understand the need—and this goes back to something that you apparently were discussing with Mr. Engel—we understand the need to provide licensing authority. It makes it more difficult to do so when an administration abuses that authority. For example, section 218 of the Iran Threat Reduction Act applied sanctions to foreign subsidiaries of U.S. companies engaging directly or indirectly with the Government of Iran.

Using that authority that we provided the administration for licensing, the Obama administration's Treasury Department issued a general license, known as General License H, in an attempt to completely circumvent these statutory prohibitions. This was clearly not the intent of Congress. And I am not saying that we should not provide the authority, but an administration must not abuse that authority that we do provide.

So would you comment on that?

Mr. SZUBIN. Yes. Thank you, Congressman, for the question. And I think you are focusing in on why this balance between the different branches is so difficult.

There is no question that Congress is given in the Constitution a key, a vital role when it comes to U.S. international commerce and there is no question that the executive branch has a key role when it comes to leading our foreign policy. And I think that over the many decades in which the two branches have been active and over the many years of sanctions laws we have seen, that is a balance that is difficult to get exactly right.

But I think Congress has had historically the right outlook on it, whether you look at the Sudan laws, whether you look at the Iran laws, the NDAA, CISADA, whether you look at things like the Refusniks issue and the Jackson-Vanik Amendment that Congress passed which put pressure on the Soviet Union to release those who were oppressed and those who weren't allowed to practice their religion in the Soviet Union.

Congress can and should put guardrails on the administration to both direct it to put more pressure on a target and to say, "You can't turn the car around without coming to Congress." I use the metaphor of guardrails. But I think it can go too far when it becomes a straitjacket.

Mr. CHABOT. Thank you.

Mr. Maltz and Mr. Zarate, I will turn to you. This is more a follow-up to the original thing I was saying.

Would you comment on the possible impact of blacklisting Iran's shipping registry for noncompliance with U.N. Security Council resolutions with respect to North Korea? Either one of you or both.

Mr. ZARATE. I think that would be highly effective, Congressman. And I think going to this question of what pressure we can put on

Iran, I think what we need to do is put full pressure on the elements of the IRGC's control over the economy. We need to demonstrate that the Iranians are engaged in nefarious behavior that is in violation of existing U.N. sanctions.

Frankly, we need to revisit parts of the deal that didn't address questions of, for example, Iranian collaboration with North Korea in the context of the nuclear program. And I think that speaks to the need to think of any agreement we have with the Iranians, the nuclear side as a living document, especially one that is to persist for 10 to 15 years.

I do want to point something out. The Iranians will claim, if we were to do exactly what you have described, which is completely legitimate and appropriate, the Iranians will claim that that is in violation of the JCPOA. And as I testified numerous times when the JCPOA was being debated, there is an inherent contradiction intentionally built into the deal.

The Iranians think they agreed and got reintegration into the global financial and commercial system. That is not what we said, obviously. We said we can apply non-nuclear sanctions as needed. But the deal itself says that the Iranians are getting reintegration into the global financial and commercial system. The very essence of the power of our sanctions is the ability to unplug them from that system.

And so there is an inherent tension in the very notion of the deal that I think we would just have to recognize. And we have to gird ourselves toward Iranian objections and maybe even European objections that if we decide to sanction the shipping lines or decide to list all of the companies that are owned and controlled by the IRGC, that are listed on the Tehran stock exchange, if we go out and enforce against what the Iranians are doing on terrorism or on other things, the Iranians are going to claim, "You are seeking the same effects as you had before, which is a campaign to financially and economically isolate us."

And the reality is that is what we are intending to do. That is not what they think they got in the deal.

Mr. CHABOT. Thank you.

Unfortunately, my time has expired, Mr. Chairman. Thank you.

Chairman ROYCE. We go to Mr. Albio Sires of New Jersey.

Mr. SIRES. Thank you, Mr. Chairman. And thank you for being here. Mr. Chairman, I wish you nothing but the best in your future endeavors.

You know, getting back to the Western Hemisphere, and I read an article a couple weeks ago about Venezuela and the horrible conditions that are there. And I am just wondering, how effective have some of the sanctions been that we have placed on Venezuela to help move it somewhere? Can anybody give me an assessment?

Mr. Zarate? On the regime, you know.

Mr. ZARATE. I think it has made the regime's life much more difficult, especially given the ability or the lack of ability of the regime to access capital and to finance some of its operations given the sanctions that we have put in place.

And this is, by the way, Congressman, where I would disagree directly with Congressman Meeks' assertion that unilateral sanctions have never worked. In the context of Venezuela sanctions, where we are far out ahead of certainly the United Nations or even the European Union, the measures we put in place to isolate those who are engaged in human rights abuses, corruption, and to deal with the ability of PDVSA and other Venezuelan key elements of the economy to access capital is actually really important.

Now, there is no question that the economic disaster that we have seen in Caracas is the effect of poor governance over the years under the Chavista regime and now under Maduro, but the sanctions we put in place I think are making it much harder for them to deal with their situation.

One other key point here, Congressman, and I think it is important for this committee, is the importance of the overlap of sanctions programs, because we tend to think of the Venezuela program here, we think of the Russia program here, the Cuba program there.

These interrelate. How we unwind our sanctions and allow the Cuban Government to access capital impacts their ability then to support the Venezuelan Government. How we think about sanctions on Rosneft, for example, which is currently subject to sectoral sanctions on the Russia program, affects the debt and equity that they are now providing, have provided, to the tune of $6 billion to PDVSA.

So we have to keep in mind and, frankly, leverage the fact that the sanctions environment and the sanctions we have in place actually overlap and give us an ability to impact the decisionmaking and, frankly, the access to capital that regimes like the Maduro government need.

Mr. SIRES. So, in your opinion, is the overlap where we can go a little bit further with sanctions?

Mr. ZARATE. Absolutely. And I think we have to be more creative about how we deal with these sanctions. I think we made a mistake in terms of how we tried to unwind the sanctions in the Cuban context in part because it relieved pressure on Cuba precisely at a time when we were putting pressure, wanted to put more pressure on Venezuela.

So these have to be viewed in concert, and we have to worry about vulnerabilities, because the Russian Government and now Rosneft have provided debt and equity financing to the Venezuelan Government, allowing them some relief from pressure. And so we have to watch to see how that ownership and control interest impacts not just in Venezuela, but even PDVSA's interests in the United States through Citgo.

Mr. SIRES. Mr. Szubin, I was curious about your comments regarding State sanctions. You don't feel that they should be, how can I say, first in implementing sanctions in some of these places? Mr. SZUBIN. Implementing sanction, absolutely. But I was talking about when State legislatures formulate their own sanctions, independently of Congress and the President, where they say, "We don't care whether Congress permits such and such activity. We are not going to allow companies in Europe or around the world to contract with us to obtain procurement or to receive investment from our State funds if they are doing such and such on the foreign stage."

And while as a general matter of course States need to be free to choose who they contract with, the objective here is a foreign policy objective. And as a result, we end up with different States pushing in different directions when it comes to America's foreign policy and I think that is a bad thing.

It has not gotten a lot of attention. I think it will in the coming years, because I think now that the States have been encouraged and allowed to go in this direction, you are going to see more of it. You see state initiatives now with respect to BDS. I can imagine a world in which you have dueling States, some who say, "We won't allow companies who have activities in the West Bank to contract with us," and others who say, "Anyone who doesn't recognize that the West Bank is a part of Israel isn't going to be allowed to contract with us."

That kind of thing should not be going on in 50 different ways across our country. I think we need to have a uniformed foreign policy and I think it has to be set here.

Mr. SIRES. Thank you, Mr. Chairman. My time is up.

Chairman ROYCE. Thank you.

I will go to Tom Marino of Pennsylvania.

Mr. MARINO. Thank you, Chairman. Thank you for your service. And, hopefully, when we are done here, we will see you at the State Department.

Gentlemen, thank you for being here.

Mr. Maltz, I want to get right to you. And if anyone wants to respond, please do so.

As an 18-year prosecutor, both at the State and at the Federal level, a U.S. attorney, I have always had the concept of "follow the money." "Follow the money" will take us to every one of those people involved, whether it is on a domestic basis or an international basis.

Mr. Maltz, what can we do, what more can we do to follow the money of those not only growing drugs and distributing, but those also producing chemicals that are used for the end product?

Now, let me give you one example quickly that I have. I was in Colombia not too long ago, and we were out in the coca fields, a helicopter went down in the fields, and saw how they were destroying "destroying coca plants." At one time they were U.S. money that we gave Colombia, were flying over the coca fields with Roundup, just a chemical that we used in our backyard to get rid of weeds.

Well, the Colombian Government stopped that, because they said they were afraid it was causing cancer. I asked one of the members that were there, "Are you not afraid of that big swimming pool size pit that you dump all the chemicals in to produce your cocaine and then it all seeps into the ground?" And he didn't want to answer me on that.

But what can we do internationally to follow the money?

Mr. MALTZ. Okay. So that is a great question. So let me answer this by saying that is exactly why I wrote a long paper on a case study to make America safer after we did the Lebanese Canadian Bank case, because it was a good model to move forward. However, we missed a lot of opportunities.

So to give you an example, like these PATRIOT Act 311 and 981(k) actions, gave us the ability to take $150 million out of an account in Lebanon. We actually ultimately forfeited $102 million in that case.

The issue is the U.S. Government needs more expertise on financial investigation. You are 100 percent correct when you talk about follow the money. The only way you are going to really shut these people down is if you take away their resources.

And that is why what you hit on is exactly my number one passion. If terrorists are turning to criminal networks for their funding, how can we have a system where the terrorist investigators in the intelligence community and others are not communicating properly with the law enforcement agencies, State and local, Federal, and have this unity of effort to put it all together?

Because it is so powerful. I was very impressed by the PATRIOT Act, just those two actions alone. And I am not an expert by any means. But I will tell you we learned from our partner at Treasury and other folks that were kind of educating us. But this is why a commingled, co-managed task force of the true experts in the country would be the most effective.

Now, I keep going back to the Counter-Narcoterrorism Operations Center we have in SOD. The reason I talk about that center is because that center was developed and because the Attorney General, the FBI Director, and the DEA Administrator said back in 2001, 2002, we need one unit that can look at the finances and the crossover, the overlap, in these particular cases.

So to really answer that—and thank you, that is a great question, and I wish that people would just focus on what you said, okay? Because if you get the right experts, like this guy and that guy, and there are people that are out there in the Beltway that can actually educate the law enforcement agents, train them.

We have some really unbelievable financial contractors right now sitting at that CNTOC in Virginia. Those are the people that follow the money around the world. I would have had no idea.

Mr. MARINO. That kind of money has to leave a trail.

Mr. MALTZ. Exactly.

Mr. MARINO. No matter where it is at. And I have worked with DEA for 18 years, one of the best agencies, I loved working with the frontline people, the men and women. But then when we brought in Treasury and other departments, we were starting to bring the cocaine trade to its knees and we just must get back to following that money.

Mr. MALTZ. One hundred percent agreed. And really anything you could do to support that in this committee, that would be one of my top recommendations, get the resources to the follow the money strategy. Get the banks—like, right now what they are really doing, which is really effective, they are actually talking to the banks like they have never done before and briefing them on these different threats. A lot of these guys are cleared former Federal people that have the clearances to be able to understand now what to look for.

Chairman ROYCE. We go to Mr. Ted Deutch of Florida.

Mr. DEUTCH. Thank you, Mr. Chairman. I want to add my voice to the many others and tell you what an honor it has been to serve under your capable leadership. And I really look forward to continuing to work with you in whatever leadership roles you have in advancing our foreign policy.

I want to refer back, gentlemen, to a speech that then-Under Secretary of Terrorism and Financial Intelligence David Cohen gave in 2014. He delivered an address about virtual currency, about cryptocurrency, and he expressed then, although he acknowledged that it was still early in the development of these currencies, he expressed then concerns about illicit finance.

He acknowledged that every year hundreds of billions of dollars of illicit funds come through the financial system—this is what you have been focused on—fundraising by terror groups, money laundering, facilitation of nuclear and ballistic missile programs, including the transfer of WMD technology proliferators. And he talked about the specific threat that cryptocurrencies posed because of the anonymity. And a lot has happened since 2014 in the advancement of bitcoin and other virtual currencies.

And I would like to hear from our panel how concerned you are about the extent to which these virtual currencies can be used for all of these illicit finance purposes and, as the New York Times reported just a week or 2 ago, can be used to avoid sanctions. In Venezuela they are talking about creating a petro, their own virtual currency, and Putin has suggested perhaps the same in Russia.

Shouldn't we be concerned that as these cryptocurrencies explode in value that it makes it easier to avoid sanctions and that it makes it easier to transfer money, weapons, weapons technology? And what do we do about it?

Mr. ZARATE. Congressman, I am happy to take first crack at this. I sit on the board of advisors for Coinbase, which, as you know, is the largest U.S.-based coin exchange operator. I have worked for them for some time and have learned quite a bit from them.

I think that we should be concerned. Any time you have access to value or the ability to move value or money across borders in a way that enables illicit actors and dangerous actors, you have to be concerned.

And you have seen examples of this. You have seen obviously in the context of ransomware the use of bitcoin as the form of payment. You have seen the Liberty Reserve, the Silk Road case, the recent enforcement action and arrests in the BTC-e case. So there are examples.

You also have the concern that you have a multiplicity of these kinds of currencies now. So it is not just bitcoin or Ethereum, but you have got a bunch of them in different platforms.

So I would be concerned, but I wouldn't be hysterical, because I think there are opportunities here and opportunities to design the technologies and platforms, especially blockchain-based platforms, to actually make them traceable, to actually leverage their ability to monitor and track the access points in a way that is very interesting. And law enforcement, I think, is drawing some attention to that. The responsible actors in the space are cooperating. And I think that is an arena of some promise.

Mr. DEUTCH. Can I follow up on that, though? You are suggesting making blockchain traceable. That is traceable by whom? You are not suggesting, are you, that—I mean, there is no oversight now, obviously, there is no Federal oversight of any of these virtual currencies. I don't believe that you are suggesting that. So who is it traceable by and how is that going to be done?

Mr. ZARATE. Well, just a correction. There is a regulation of exchange operators that act as money service businesses. So they are subject to the same regulations and requirements as a money service business, a Western Union, et cetera. So that is one thing. There is regulation and European authorities and others are putting regulation in place.

The second point is I am talking about the legitimate adoption of the underlying technology that allows for payment, trade, finance, et cetera, that actually allows you to create within a closed system the ability to track who is involved, who is in and out of the system, and to define what is a legitimate transaction in the context of that blockchain platform. That is something the major global banks are exploring now, that is something that even central banks are exploring with their own currencies.

But I think your point about the systemic risk is a good one, an important one, because we see Russia doing this, we see Venezuela doing this, trying to explore these as alternatives to the dollar.

Mr. DEUTCH. If I could just ask, Mr. Szubin, do you share the concerns that your predecessor raised back then? And do you believe that having the identifying—finding ways to make these traceable will work without the absence of some role of the Federal Government?

Mr. SZUBIN. I do share the concerns, I share the concerns that Mr. Zarate is raising. I think we need to have the same standards when it comes to transparency and reporting suspicious activity for virtual currencies as we do for regular currencies, for fiat currencies. It is as simple as that.

And our regulatory system is strong. I think it is very well thought out, well designed. We just need to be holding anyone who is moving value, in regardless of what form it is, to the same standards.

Mr. MALTZ. Which we don't do now.

Mr. SZUBIN. Well, FinCEN actually has, and it has said that if you are moving money, whether it is virtual currency or fiat currency, you are a money exchanger and you are responsible to report and file in the same way that a Western Union has.

Mr. DEUTCH. Mr. Chairman, before I yield back.

If you are right, that is for the good actors. And I hope perhaps we can have a hearing in the future about how it is that a terror group, for example, can utilize a virtual currency in order to acquire, in the worst case scenario, plutonium, WMD materials. That is, I think, a very serious concern that we should have and that I hope we can explore further.

Chairman ROYCE. And I think Mr. Deutch makes a very valid recommendation here to me and Mr. Engel and we will do a hearing on that subject. Thank you.

We now go to Mr. Ted Yoho of Florida.

Mr. YOHO. Thank you, Mr. Chairman. And I ditto all those kind things everybody said about you.

Mr. Szubin, let me ask you, because you are talking about preserving our financial system, the Western currency or the U.S.

market. People want that because it follows the rule of law, it can be tracked, it is an honest way of doing business, as Mr. Deutch brought up. The good actors want that. It is the bad actors that we have to worry about.

And then I worry about how much pressure can we use with the sanctions and how far can you go. And you said you weren't in favor of the secondary sanctions so much on maybe businesses.

But when you have a situation like what is going on in North Korea, and we have Chinese companies or shell companies going through Hong Kong. I think I read an article not too long ago there are over 140 shell companies that were doing business for the sake of North Korea, but they weren't North Korean, and a lot of that money was going through China.

So at what point do you go after the secondary or maybe even the tertiary from the government—up to the government and put that pressure on there?

And the last thing I want to do is to put so much pressure where people don't want to use our system and we fall into the hands of Putin and they go to some other, which I hope I never see.

How far can you go?

Mr. SZUBIN. That is a critical question, Congressman. And I tried to be careful in how I phrased my concerns about secondary sanctions. I did not say we shouldn't ever use them. I think they were used to tremendous effect in the Iran case.

Mr. YOHO. Right.

Mr. SZUBIN. And what I said is they should be used exceedingly rarely. We just have to be very careful and know what we are doing before we deploy them. When you talk about North Korea, that is a threat of the first order, in my view.

Mr. YOHO. Right. That is a world threat.

Mr. SZUBIN. And I think it absolutely warrants the use of secondary sanctions. Forgive me if I wasn't clear about that. I want to be clear about that.

Mr. YOHO. Okay. I just wanted to clarify. Because we have seen what China has not done. We have seen them be complicit with this. We have seen Russia. We have seen other nations. I think it is time that we have to do it.

But as somebody else brought up, we can't do it unilaterally. We have to have the world buy into this. And with the 16 nations that voted unanimously against North Korea to put these sanctions, we have to come together as a world community and do that for the sake of humanity, I think, with the weapons that are on the table.

Let me move over to Mr. Zarate. You were talking about weeding the garden with all your different tools when you get into sanctions and things like that. I come from an agrarian background and we use manual labor, you know, pulling them out, as I remember as a kid. You can burn it, you can use herbicides, fungicides, whatever you need to.

What other tools do you need? And I think, Mr. Maltz, you brought this up too. We have plenty of agencies, we coordinate these, we don't need another agency or clearinghouse.

But on the IT side, with China, again, advancing and Russia advancing ahead of us, or neck and neck, with artificial intelligence and moving into quantum computing, are we behind on that? Do we not have the technology? And if we don't, it just irritates the stew out of me, because we should be leading that.

What are your thoughts on that? Where do we focus?

Mr. ZARATE. Yeah, Congressman, I think the first point is a critical one, which is we have to use all our tools, especially in critical cases like North Korea. So we need to be using law enforcement, financial regulations, sanctions, diplomacy, all of it in terms of identifying the vulnerability that North Korea has and then going after and weeding them out.

But in terms of information sharing, you are absolutely right, I think we are behind the curve. And we are behind the curve in a couple ways, and I described it earlier.

One is, I think we are behind in trying to figure out ways of applying new technologies to aggregate and analyze data on a real-time basis. So, for example, some countries, like Australia and Canada, pull in the data on cross-border wire information, the things coming in and out of their financial system. We obviously don't do that. The volumes are too high, there are privacy issues, of course.

But we are not even near that. We are in a 20th century analog system in terms of waiting for reports from banks, 90 to 120 days, right?

Mr. YOHO. Right. We are operating on DOS.

Mr. ZARATE. And to Derek's point earlier, there is a hunger in the private sector to actually be more collaborative, because it helps them prioritize, they want to share information. And so we have to be creative internally as well as with the private sector.

Mr. YOHO. What I would like to do is reach out to you individually, if we can, and how we can build sanctions provisions in the blockchains, as was brought up, and Mr. Deutch did a good job on that.

I am going to run out of time here. Mr. Maltz, do you have anything you want to add into that?

Mr. MALTZ. I want to add something very important. When we talk about bitcoin——

Mr. YOHO. You are from northeast Mobile, right?

Mr. MALTZ. Yes, sir, New York.

I will tell you that I witnessed firsthand the amazing capabilities of the United States Government agencies crushing Silk Road and AlphaBay. Okay? These are the most sophisticated sites in bitcoin and cryptocurrencies, but when you put the best and brightest together and share the lessons learned and these techniques, we are unstoppable. So put them together. That is the key.

Mr. YOHO. Okay. Appreciate it.

I am out of time. Thank you, Mr. Chairman.

Chairman ROYCE. Thank you.

We go to Robin Kelly of Illinois.

Ms. KELLY. Thank you, Mr. Chair. And I want to add my voice to the chorus and thank you for all of your wonderful service to the United States and to this committee. Thank you.

Thank you, Mr. Chairman and Ranking Member, for holding this hearing on sanctions and financial pressure. The U.S. has sought to use targeted sanctions against countries that violate international norms and undermine U.S. interests. Following Putin's annexation of Crimea and invasion of Ukraine, the U.S. has sanctioned Russia under numerous bills, including the Countering America's Adversaries Through Sanctions Act. Altogether, the U.S. has sanctioned over 600 persons with close coordination between State and Treasury.

These sanctions have had a real impact on the Russian economy. Following the 2014 sanctions, Russia went into a recession, with the value of the ruble plummeting and capital flight compounding a drop in oil prices.

Mr. Szubin, one of the reasons that sanctions were so successful with Iran was our close coordination with the European Union. What type of coordination is there between the U.S. and the EU during sanction development? And how can the U.S. improve coordination with our allies to apply maximum pressure on countries like Russia that undermine U.S. interests?

Mr. SZUBIN. That is probably the issue I spent more time on in my years at Treasury than any other. People think about doing sanctions as drafting up the sanctions, figuring out who the targets are, enforcing them, going after violators. That is all true and that is all a part of it. But building the international consensus takes a lot of patient work. It is not easy, but it is vital. Because as you point out, we don't succeed if we act alone when we have threats that are global.

And the European Union has been a stalwart ally when it comes to the Russia sanctions. They have hung tough. It hasn't been easy for them. They have to get consensus from 28 member states. Every 6 months, all 28 have to agree to keep those sanctions in effect, which is a very challenging juggling act for the European Union. But they have done so when it came to the Ukraine and Crimea-focused sanctions and I give them a lot of credit for that. But we need them when it comes to election interference. Putin has threatened European elections just as much as he has threatened elections here. And I think he needs to be held to account for that.

Ms. KELLY. I think the Prime Minister of England spoke about that and then the President of France. I just saw something about them mentioning Russia in their elections.

The Countering America's Adversaries Through Sanctions Act gave the Trump administration flexibility to enforce sanctions against Russia, yet the Trump administration appears to be quite restrained in their use of their authorities.

What next steps do you think Congress should take to ensure that the administration is properly enforcing CAATSA as Congress intended? And how should OFAC be strengthened or modernized to increase its efficiency and interagency collaboration?

Mr. SZUBIN. In terms of next steps under CAATSA, Congress has set out an aggressive timetable for administration action, and I think the ball is right it now in the administration's court. There is a deadline coming up at the end of month for the administration to come forward with additional names, I think an additional report to Congress. So I think that is where the attention now is.

And I think Congress' focus on this has, frankly, been very helpful. It has been bipartisan. And I think the sanctions work so much better when Congress acts in a bipartisan fashion.

When you talk about strengthening OFAC, it harkens back to comments that the chairman made and that I included in my written testimony. We are asking so much out of this little office. Whether it is organized crime, narcotics, terrorism, Syria, Russia, Iran, Venezuela, you name it, we are asking this office to track down the bad guys and put economic pressure on them. And I think having Congress' support in getting additional resources would be incredibly helpful.

Ms. KELLY. Thank you.

Mr. Maltz, as a native New Yorker, I love how you sound.

I yield back.

Mr. MALTZ. Thank you.

Ms. KELLY. I yield back.

Chairman ROYCE. Ann Wagner, Missouri.

Mrs. WAGNER. Thank you, Mr. Chairman. We are all grateful for your service to our Nation and look forward with anticipation to the future and how we can be supportive.

I am grateful that you hosted this important hearing on sanctions tools. I had the privilege of visiting South Korea and China this August after voting for the Korean Interdiction and Modernization of Sanctions Act. And I am pleased that the administration had begun implementing secondary sanction on banks and companies that are facilitating trade with North Korea and I look forward to finding ways to address North Korea's sanctions evasions practices in 2018.

Mr. Zarate, do you believe that the Trump administration's initial secondary sanction here that we talked about in 2017 have been useful in altering China's financial calculous? And then, looking on, what is it that you are looking for in 2018 from the administration?

Mr. ZARATE. Congresswoman, I think the mere threat of secondary sanctions is effective in terms of sensitizing the Chinese to the risks of continuing to do business with North Korea the way they have been.

And I think the sense of urgency and the sword of Damocles of the secondary sanctions has been very effective actually in changing the landscape. You have seen U.N. Security Council resolutions that have been tougher, you have seen better compliance from the Chinese—not perfect by any stretch—especially in terms of the mineral and coal trade. You have seen greater interdictions, we have seen two recently from the South Koreans, in terms of maritime concerns.

And so I would say that the mere threat of secondary sanctions conditions the marketplace, and especially for those, for example, Chinese banks that want to operate in the United States. The legitimate actors realize they have to comply with U.S. laws and international norms.

The more we can sensitize the environment, the better off we are. And the use of things like section 311, as was used against Dandong Bank, becomes very important to signal to the market where are the risks and what should you stay away from.

Mrs. WAGNER. I was in Dandong when that sanction came down and watching the trade back and forth, and I think it has been effective.

Mr. Maltz, I appreciate your willingness to speak out on the Obama administration's obstruction of justice regarding Project Cassandra. The U.S. has a clear national security obligation to respond to Hezbollah's criminal and terrorist activities.

To what extent can the Trump administration reverse the damage of the last 8 years and issue indictments against Hezbollah agents.

Mr. MALTZ. Again, going back to the fundamental point I have been saying all morning, is information sharing at 100 percent, break down the damn walls between the terror and the crime investigators, okay? Provide the financial experts what they need and the resources.

And to answer the other question about IT, we are in the Dark Ages and we need to upgrade those systems of collaboration and information sharing.

But the thing is, is that we have to remember that prosecutions pursuant to the rule of law are powerful, and if you look back over time there weren't that many. As soon as you raise the name Hezbollah, it is a terrorist group. Well, no, they are international criminals, they are transnational criminals that are trying to destroy our country.

Mrs. WAGNER. That is right.

Mr. MALTZ. So you must pull together your experts in every area. It is not one thing. And that is where we have to really change our culture and thought process, and folks in this room can help do that.

Mrs. WAGNER. Well, I hope that the U.S. agencies have learned some lessons, like Homeland Security and DOJ.

Mr. MALTZ. No. They have not learned because——

Mrs. WAGNER. And I question that. Project Cassandra is a perfect example of those walls being built up between and they have not moved forward.

Mr. MALTZ. Like I have said over and over again, and think about this, put your taxpayer hat on, when we did that action, we actually identified hundreds of used car businesses in America sending cars to West Africa. We only included 30 in the 311 action and the civil complaint because of limited sharing. Okay? So that is unacceptable, and when it somebody going to be held accountable for that?

Mrs. WAGNER. Thank you.

In my limited time, Mr. Zarate, do you believe that the 2017 U.N. sanctions will effectively cut into North Korea's profits from forced labor outside its borders?

Mr. ZARATE. I think so, and it was long overdue to cut off that source of funding. I think we have to put more diplomatic pressure on those countries that continue to host the guest workers because money continues to flow back. That is a source of revenue.

And, Congresswoman, to your point about criminality, in the context of North Korea they give us a gift. This is a criminal Mafia state that engages in smuggling, money laundering, human rights abuses, sanctions evasion, abuse of the financial system. So this is the prime target to use the kinds of financial measures and tools that we have talked about and that work so well against Iran.

Mrs. WAGNER. Thank you.

My time has expired, Mr. Chairman. I yield back.

Chairman ROYCE. Brad Schneider of Illinois.

Mr. SCHNEIDER. Thank you, Mr. Chairman. And I too want to associate myself with the many remarks commending you for your service and wishing you well in your future. You will be very, very much missed.

And I want to thank the witnesses.

In my limited time I want to, in a second, talk about the strategic application of sanctions, but first I want to touch on the concerns with our elections. Others have mentioned them before.

Last year, or now in 2017, U.S. intelligence agencies found that Russia did in fact interfere in the 2016 election, and there is no doubt in my mind that they are going to seek to do it again this year. And I fear that the current administration's apparent lack of resolve to secure our next election is giving Russia an even greater opportunity to achieve some mischief.

I also serve, in addition to the Foreign Affairs Committee, on the Judiciary Committee. And I had the opportunity to raise this question with the Attorney General, Deputy Attorney General, and FBI Director. And I will be honest, their answers left me more concerned that the United States isn't necessarily taking this threat seriously, and isn't doing what we need to do to secure our elections.

In the time since Congress passed CAATSA earlier in the summer last year very few authorities for Russian sanctions have been used. Mr. Szubin, you mentioned that there were sanctions in 2016. But specifically we haven't got there.

My question to the panel is, do you believe our apparent reluctance to move forward, our resistance to apply these sanctions is emboldening Russia to take more actions against our elections in the coming year?

Mr. ZARATE. Congressman, I don't have access to intelligence or information to be able to assess what the reaction of the Kremlin is. But I think we certainly have to apply whatever national measures we have and pressure to deter actors, be it the Russians, the Chinese, the North Koreans, the Iranians, from doing anything to affect our systems and our national economy, and certainly our electoral system as a critical infrastructure. So I am a firm believer of that.

This is also where the Russians are giving us a gift by what they are trying to do to evade sanctions and pressure, where they are working with the North Koreans, according to open source reporting, to provide cyber access. That is a real problem, because the North Koreans have attacked Sony, they have engaged in cyber hacking of the Bank of Bangladesh, they have engaged in a whole host of things that we need to be worried about.

And so it is not just about what happened in the prior election, it is about the threats that are coming, and it is where the Russians, North Koreans, Iranians are doing some real damage in cyberspace. And we have to apply all the tools we can to deter that activity.

Mr. SCHNEIDER. I couldn't agree more. We have to understand what happened in the past, and apply it to lessons in the future so they don't succeed.

Mr. Szubin, if you want to add anything briefly.

Mr. SZUBIN. I agree wholeheartedly. I would only add on top of that this has to be more than just a U.S.-Russia issue. Russia's activities to interfere with elections have gone to other key democracies, to our allies.

All democratic governments need to stand up to this and act as one. It is no less of a threat, to my mind, than is terrorism, than is nuclear proliferation, because it is a threat to such a core element of our system. It goes to citizens having confidence that their elected leaders really are their elected leaders. So I think we have to be very stalwart in this.

If I could Congressman, I just wanted to say one thing in response to the assertions from Mrs. Wagner, from Congresswoman Wagner, when it comes to the last administration's activities on Hezbollah. Because I sat in a chair and I had at least a role when it came to going after Hezbollah, Hezbollah's financing in the last administration.

And we were not sitting on our hands in any way. We issued dozens of designations against Hezbollah facilitators and officers. There were the indictments and forfeitures that Mr. Maltz referred to earlier against Lebanese Canadian Bank, against the Jemaah network. There were 311 actions against money exchange houses in Lebanon. All of this from the years 2013 through 2016 during the Iran negotiations.

So I saw no effort to slow. In fact, I saw quite a lot to encourage action against Hezbollah and against Hezbollah financing.

Mr. SCHNEIDER. And I will share in 2014, with the help of the chairman and ranking member, and with my colleague Mark Meadows, we drafted the Hezbollah International Financing Prevention Act in legislation that ultimately passed, and became law. We have to do everything we can to make sure Hezbollah doesn't have the ability to project and raise their resources around the world through criminal activity, drug activity, and then in the region as an agent of Iran.

I am out of time. I will say one more thing and I will follow up with written questions. But I think it is important you touched on the strategic application of sanctions as, Mr. Zarate, you said, a tool in the space between diplomacy and kinetic action. I think that is important to understand.

But I think it is important to understand that these have to be driven by our national interests and our subsequent strategic goals and principles, which you all have laid out, and that they are constrained by the limits of our influence, relationships, reach, and resources.

So I have more questions, I don't have time. But I will say it is important for our committee, for this Congress to make sure that we provide the resources, the consistency, follow the principles, and that for our administration and our Nation to continue to work to build the relationships.

I am very concerned about cuts to our State Department, and the deemphasizing of diplomacy. Without that diplomacy, without the ability to reach out to our allies to apply sanctions, sanctions which have a half-life over time so we need to continually ratchet them up, that our ability to use this important tool will be diminished in the future.

So I will follow up. But thank you for your time.

And with that, I yield back.

Chairman ROYCE. Thank you.

We go to Mr. Lee Zeldin of New York.

Mr. ZELDIN. Thank you, Chairman. Congratulations on your retirement. Thank you for your incredible service. And I wish you the best of luck with everything that is ahead. Now when we visit you in the State Department, I hear that we will actually be visiting Marie. So congratulations there.

Mr. Szubin, if I understand a couple of your comments over the course of this hearing correctly, it is your belief that Iran is abiding by its end of the JCPOA?

Mr. SZUBIN. The consensus, to my mind, is that Iran is abiding by all of its commitments, all of its material commitments under the JCPOA, yes.

Mr. ZELDIN. So I will put this nicely, but maybe before the next time you appear before Congress, some items I would ask for you and some of your other former colleagues to look into before reiterating that again: Iran stockpiling more heavy water than they are supposed to; acquiring more IR-6 rotor assemblies than they are allowed to under the JCPOA; spinning more IR-8 assemblies than they are allowed to under the JCPOA; saying unequivocally they will not allow any access to any of their military sites; attempting to acquire carbon fiber that they are not allowed to; conducting mechanical testing of advanced centrifuges that they are not allowed to; refusing IAEA access to Sharif University; possessing chemically manmade particles of natural uranium.

There was that one inspection of Parchin that showed the manmade particles. There was no follow-up allowed, no further access.

So I can ask you to comment on all that. It is really important because there are a lot of people coming before Congress and to the American public and saying that Iran is abiding by its own end of the nuclear deal, and it is really important that all these violations of the letter of the deal are factored in before making that statement.

Going back to your time with the administration, what is your understanding of the relationship between Iran and al-Qaeda?

Mr. SZUBIN. I want to be careful to respect any information that I learned from classified sources. Obviously, I wouldn't be able to speak to that in an open setting.

But my understanding historically has been that Iran was willing to tolerate a physical al-Qaeda presence on their soil and there was something of a quid pro quo there.

So we actually at Treasury designated a number of al-Qaeda officials and pinpointed their location as being in Iran at the time of the designation. So to describe it as a place where al-Qaeda has found some safe haven would, to my mind, be accurate.

Mr. ZELDIN. And I very much appreciate your assessment, which I completely agree with, it was July 28th of 2011 that you made that designation. The raid of the bin Laden compound was May 2011. So the administration quickly assessed those documents, Treasury made that designation.

There have been terms used like viewing Iran as a main artery or a core pipeline between in correspondence, documents that were gotten from that, received from that raid between al-Qaeda and Iraq, and al-Qaeda, bin Laden, and the rest of the operation in Afghanistan and Southeast Asia. So I really do appreciate you saying that.

There are some contradictory statements that have been made during this timeline. So between the May 2011 raid, the July 28, 2011, Treasury designation, and us having this conversation today, there would be comments used like saying it is a baseless conspiracy theory, what we are talking about here. There were officials who said, "Anyone who thinks Iran was or is in bed with al-Qaeda doesn't know much about either."

So that is another issue that I think it is very helpful that you are here and making the statement that you did, because there clearly was an active relationship between Iran and al-Qaeda that was greatly concerning. It was an active relationship right up until the time of that raid.

For the public's awareness, they are becoming increasingly more aware of a decision to release 470,000 documents that were collected in that raid that weren't previously released before a few months ago, which is a decision that I strongly support.

I appreciate all three of our witnesses being here for today's testimony.

Chairman, again, best wishes—well, he is not here anymore.

But, Chairman McCaul, I will yield back.

Mr. SZUBIN. If I could, though, Congressman, just very briefly, I think you are right that the situation here has involved connections between al-Qaeda and Iran over the years. And you are right to point that out.

I do see accusations that are a lot more sweeping and to my mind inaccurate. And so I think what is called for is just real precision and accuracy in what we are describing.

Iran hasn't been a major funder, we never saw Iran pumping money to al-Qaeda. There are a number of other Sunni countries have been a lot more problematic when it came to charities and fundraising for al-Qaeda than Iran, which is of course a Shia country.

So I don't want to whitewash their behavior when it has come to al-Qaeda. In fact, at Treasury we were involved in helping to call it out. I just think we need to be precise and accurate in how we describe those relationships.

Mr. ZELDIN. Right. And, again, it gets back to really, on both sides, on all sides, of analyzing this argument, because there were some people in the prior administration who were referring to this as a baseless conspiracy theory, what we are referring to, which is contradicting reality.

And I think with regards to Iran offering financing and arms, the documents are showing more of an offer than what you are seeing as far as evidence of them actually providing financing and arms. But certainly a relationship and an artery.

And I do yield back now. Thank you, Chairman.

Mr. MCCAUL [presiding]. The Chair now recognizes Mrs. Norma Torres.

Mrs. TORRES. Thank you, Mr. Chairman.

Mr. Zarate, last year I introduced the North Korea Follow the Money Act. The bill requires a national intelligence estimate on North Korea's revenue sources. This information is very important to ensure that our sanctions are effective.

How confident are you that our North Korea sanctions are hitting the right targets? And do we know enough about this regime, how it operates, to actually be effective?

Mr. ZARATE. Congresswoman, first of all, thank you for that piece of legislation and your focus on trying to understand the financial networks of North Korea, because one of the challenges in this space has been the assumption that the Hermit Kingdom doesn't have economic or commercial vulnerabilities or capital. And that is completely wrong. They have relationships with banks. They have trading relationships. They have relied on forced labor in Western countries.

And so mapping out their relationships and their dependencies is really important. We can never know enough about this regime. And I think one of the things we don't know enough about is how the regime leadership itself controls its own money, where it may have it even outside of the country.

But I think we have done a better job of understanding its relationships with China, and in particular its trading relationship in Dandong. And I think the focus on the mineral trade is incredibly important.

We have learned more, in particular, from nongovernmental sources how the North Koreans are using their shipping and proliferation to raise money. We know more about the volume in terms of the human rights abuses and the slave labor in parts around the world.

And so we have a better tableau. And I think congressional legislation, the U.N. sanctions, have targeted on those vulnerabilities.

The challenge is the North Koreans adapt. They adapted after Banco Delta Asia in 2006, which was, by the way, to Congressman Meeks' points earlier, a unilateral U.S. step that had global impact to isolate BDA at the time.

But they will adapt. And they also then find areas of vulnerability in order to make money, to include now cyber. And you see the North Koreans now investing more resources in trying to find cyber vulnerabilities and to profit from it.

Mrs. TORRES. Right.

Bringing it back to the Western Hemisphere, Mr. Szubin, as you know, right before Christmas, we saw the first Global Magnitsky sanctions come out. And I was very pleased and encouraged that a political figure from Guatemala was included in that list.

Guatemala, as you know, is an ally of the U.S., and we are doing a lot of important work, investing taxpayers' dollars in infrastructure in the Northern Triangle. In Guatemala we are working very closely with the attorney general and CICIG. And as the founder and co-chair of the Central America Caucus, I have been very supportive of the work that they are doing in dealing with public corruption.

But the political class and many individuals in the private sector have been doing a lot of work and a lot of damage to undermine the work of CICIG and the attorney general. I think we need to send a stronger message to those actors from the U.S.

So what are our options for expanding targeted sanctions in a country like Guatemala that is so dependent on the U.S.?

Mr. SZUBIN. Thank you, Congresswoman.

I think the approach that you are describing is exactly the right one, work with those aspects of the society and the government that are for clean government, that are trying to serve their citizens, and try to marginalize or put pressure on those who are forces of corruption and of regression.

Targeted sanctions can be a part of that strategy. And I am glad, as you say, that we have seen the administration harnessing that tool.

I am no longer inside government, so I can't speak with any expertise as to where additional opportunities might lie, but I think that is a great conversation for you to have with my former office.

Mrs. TORRES. Right. It is troubling to me when the Vice President of that country makes a comment that if we are going—the U.S. is going to begin to impose sanctions on specific individuals, that they would be targeting every Guatemalan in country because they are all guilty of being corrupt at one point or another. I was born in Guatemala, and I took that as a very offensive comment that he would make toward people that he was elected to represent.

More troubling is the fact that it has been so difficult for the U.S. to begin this process of ensuring that a country that we are investing so much in is able to produce the judges and to produce the legislative branch for themselves that they need in order to bring to trial some of these very bad actors.

Thank you, and I yield back.

Mr. MCCAUL. The gentlelady yields back.

The Chair recognizes himself for 5 minutes for questions.

Thank you for being here today. I just have a couple of questions. First, Iran. Ranking Member Eliot Engel and I visited Israel. The prime minister talked about the Shia Crescent, the movement into Iraq and Syria. We are seeing some very aggressive movements by Iran now in that region. I think also the lifting of the sanctions, I think a lot of that money is going into criminal enterprise now and terror organizations, Hezbollah being one of them. I think ISIS is spreading now to Africa, northern Africa. And I think Iran, as Mr. Zeldin pointed out, has had a very odd relationship with al-Qaeda and Sunni forces as well. And I think that transnational organization trade out of Africa into the Western Hemisphere is real and the tri-border area where I have been is real, and that puts it right in our backyard.

And, I guess, Mr. Maltz, your experience with DEA, I mean, are we making any progress to stop the flow of this transnational criminal organization that Iran has been supporting?

Mr. MALTZ. We have made progress. I mean, that is why I wrote a long paper about the whole Lebanese Canadian Bank and some of the stuff that we did.

However, we have so much work to do. They are working hard right now in these operations, and I know that they are going to have some more success.

However, we will never make the progress that you are looking for if we don't get the expertise together. We have to have the unity of effort, like the strategy under Obama called for, President Obama. And under President Trump it is the same words. But the words are no good. You need the action. You need the experts together.

And until that happens, we are going to be talking about this and hopefully nothing catastrophic happens. I mean, like I said, 2008, Michael Chertoff made it clear, Hezbollah makes al-Qaeda look like the minor leagues, right? Jim Stavridis with his fireball slide, when Islamic narcoterrorists and extremists get together, that is a very bad nightmare. General Kelly has testified so many times about this emergence down in South America, Central America, the tri-border region, cocaine flowing into the Middle East. Money is being made all over.

So until we get our teams together and hold people accountable, we are going to be talking about this forever.

Mr. MCCAUL. As you know, I was a Federal prosecutor in counterterrorism. I remember one of the first cases in the United States was actually a cigarette/baby milk case from Hezbollah.

Mr. MALTZ. Well, it is funny you say that, because right now I am, like, obsessing over this ongoing problem with illegal cigarette trafficking, EBT fraud, drug paraphernalia, synthetic drugs. All these different smaller type crimes coming together, commingling in one place, and then moneys being sent through our financial system to Yemen, as an example.

So until we get our experts to share that intelligence, sit in a room, break down the walls, we are going to be talking about this for a long time.

Mr. MCCAUL. Well, and I think we have now, I think, reinforced our alliance with Israel, and now with the Saudis. So, hopefully, the enemy—your enemy is Iran, and hopefully they can provide some assistance.

Mr. Zarate, I know we had a meeting in my office, and I have a conflict so we will have to reschedule. But for now I wanted to ask you the question really about sanctions. I mean, we lifted a lot of the sanctions in Iran. I had my differences with that position. As I look at the IRGC, which is really the terror arm—and Hezbollah too—the terror arm of Iran, would it be effective, sanctions, can sanctions be effective against them? What is your position on the utility of designating organizations like this a foreign terror organization?

Mr. ZARATE. Mr. Chairman, thank you. And I am sorry to miss you later, but it is great to see you again.

Mr. MCCAUL. You too.

Mr. ZARATE. I think the designations are fine. The designations allow for authorities. The question is, what follows next?

I think in the context of Iran and IRGC there are two huge advantages that we have. The IRGC, as you said, is the centerpiece of human rights abuses, support to terrorist proxies through the Quds Force, engaging in criminality with Hezbollah, and the center of gravity politically. They are also the center of gravity economically, along with the bonyads that the supreme leader and the clerics control.

So that means they are a criminal state. They are a terror-sponsoring state. And what you can do is economically isolate them in a way, akin to what we did in the nuclear context, through the use of sanctions and financial isolation by using sanctions, prosecutions, and all the full weight of things that we can do to isolate them from the formal financial and commercial system.

That then affects the marketplace. This the why the Iranians have not felt relief. It is why they don't have transparency in their financial system. It is why they are having the riots in the streets. And it is precisely where we have a strategic lever that we can use. As I said earlier, the Iranians are going to squawk any time we try to do this kind of measure because they will argue that we are trying to reimpose the nuclear sanctions. We should be very clear about what the purpose of this is, and we should then enlist our allies in Europe and the rest of the world who care about human rights, who care about terrorism, who care about the issues we care about, to actually follow our lead. And so I think that is critical.

A final point, and this is in my testimony, and I didn't mention it earlier but it is really important. To have OFAC and the financial regulators focusing on ownership and control interest is really important. This is where the market reacts to what is owned and control and what is the financial infrastructure and base for these organizations and these parties.

We do a pretty good job of that currently, the U.S. Government, but not as good a job as we should. And you now have private sector organizations like FDD, C4ADS, and others that are trying to put out lists of the things that the North Koreans own and control, the things that IRGC controls. That is really important.

So it is not just the designation at the top level as a criminal organization or a terrorist organization. It is what follows next. What do they own and control? And what can we isolate under principles that the international community understands?

Mr. MCCAUL. Thank you.

I just was notified we have about 3 minutes left on the clock for votes. I know, Ms. Titus, you are last but not least. But if we could make it a little brief, because I would like to make the votes. And thank you.

Ms. TITUS. Thank you, Mr. Chairman. I will be brief.

We have heard a lot about the importance or the effectiveness of sanctions. But I question just how well they work if the administration is only kind of halfheartedly behind them.

When CAATSA was passed overwhelmingly by this body, bipartisan, the President expressed concerns. He was reluctant to sign it. He got threatened with a veto override, and then he agreed to go along with it.

But I wonder, Mr. Szubin, if you think that his public reluctance on the legislation, his slowness to implement the sanctions, missing deadlines, if that doesn't undermine their effectiveness and Russia just doesn't take them very seriously. You said sanctions are like guardrails on the highway that allow us to adjust speed. Do you think it is time for this administration to adjust its speed?

Mr. SZUBIN. Well, I, first of all, agree with the premise of your question. Sanctions don't work if they are not very vigorously enforced. And the reason our sanctions have been able to have impact where they have is because companies in the U.S. and around the world know and fear our enforcement regime.

With respect to CAATSA, I think we have to watch what the administration does. So a key deadline is coming up at the end of this month, and I expect Congress, and among them yourself and this committee, will be watching to see how aggressively the administration implements the new law.

Ms. TITUS. Thank you.

Mr. McCAUL. Thank you for your brevity.

I want to thank the witnesses for your excellent testimony on sanctions and the way we can use law enforcement to effectuate our national security. And I think your testimony will help us in that effort. So, again, thank you.

And this committee now stands adjourned.

[Whereupon, at 12:25 p.m., the committee was adjourned.]

APPENDIX

Material Submitted for the Record

FULL COMMITTEE HEARING NOTICE
COMMITTEE ON FOREIGN AFFAIRS
U.S. HOUSE OF REPRESENTATIVES
WASHINGTON, DC 20515-6128

Edward R. Royce (R-CA), Chairman

January 10, 2018

TO: MEMBERS OF THE COMMITTEE ON FOREIGN AFFAIRS

You are respectfully requested to attend an OPEN hearing of the Committee on Foreign Affairs to be held in Room 2172 of the Rayburn House Office Building (and available live on the Committee website at http://www.ForeignAffairs.house.gov):

DATE: Wednesday, January 10, 2018

TIME: 10:00 a.m.

SUBJECT: Sanctions and Financial Pressure: Major National Security Tools

WITNESSES: The Honorable Juan C. Zarate
Chairman and Co-Founder
Financial Integrity Network
(*Former Assistant Secretary for Terrorist Financing and Financial Crimes, U.S. Department of the Treasury*)

Mr. Derek Maltz
Executive Director
Governmental Relations
Pen-Link, Ltd.
(*Former Special Agent in Charge, Special Operations Division, Drug Enforcement Administration, U.S. Department of Justice*)

Mr. Adam Szubin
Distinguished Practitioner-in-Residence
Johns Hopkins University School of Advanced International Studies
(*Former Acting Under Secretary for Terrorism and Financial Intelligence, U.S. Department of the Treasury*)

By Direction of the Chairman

The Committee on Foreign Affairs seeks to make its facilities accessible to persons with disabilities. If you are in need of special accommodations, please call 202/225-5021 at least four business days in advance of the event, whenever practicable. Questions with regard to special accommodations in general (including availability of Committee materials in alternative formats and assistive listening devices) may be directed to the Committee.

COMMITTEE ON FOREIGN AFFAIRS
MINUTES OF FULL COMMITTEE HEARING

Day __Wednesday__ Date __01/10/2018__ Room __2172__

Starting Time __10:06AM__ Ending Time __12:25PM__

Recesses __0__ (___to___)(___to___)(___to___)(___to___)(___to___)(___to___)

Presiding Member(s)
Chairman Edward R. Royce   Representative Michael McCaul
Representative Ileana Ros-Lehtinen

Check all of the following that apply:

Open Session ☑   Electronically Recorded (taped) ☑
Executive (closed) Session ☐   Stenographic Record ☑
Televised ☑

TITLE OF HEARING:

Sanctions and Financial Pressure: Major National Security Tools

COMMITTEE MEMBERS PRESENT:

See attached.

NON-COMMITTEE MEMBERS PRESENT:

N/A

HEARING WITNESSES: Same as meeting notice attached? Yes ☑ No ☐
(If "no", please list below and include title, agency, department, or organization.)

STATEMENTS FOR THE RECORD: *(List any statements submitted for the record.)*

IFR - Representative Steve Chabot
SFR - Representative Gerry Connolly
QFR - Representative William Keating

TIME SCHEDULED TO RECONVENE __________
or
TIME ADJOURNED __12:25PM__

Full Committee Hearing Coordinator

HOUSE COMMITTEE ON FOREIGN AFFAIRS
FULL COMMITTEE HEARING

PRESENT	MEMBER
X	Edward R. Royce, CA
X	Christopher H. Smith, NJ
X	Ileana Ros-Lehtinen, FL
X	Dana Rohrabacher, CA
X	Steve Chabot, OH
X	Joe Wilson, SC
X	Michael T. McCaul, TX
	Ted Poe, TX
	Darrell Issa, CA
X	Tom Marino, PA
X	Mo Brooks, AL
	Paul Cook, CA
X	Scott Perry, PA
X	Ron DeSantis, FL
	Mark Meadows, NC
X	Ted Yoho, FL
	Adam Kinzinger, IL
X	Lee Zeldin, NY
X	Dan Donovan, NY
	James F. Sensenbrenner, Jr., WI
X	Ann Wagner, MO
	Brian J. Mast, FL
X	Brian K. Fitzpatrick, PA
	Francis Rooney, FL
	Thomas A. Garrett, Jr., VA
X	John Curtis, UT

PRESENT	MEMBER
X	Eliot L. Engel, NY
X	Brad Sherman, CA
X	Gregory W. Meeks, NY
X	Albio Sires, NJ
X	Gerald E. Connolly, VA
X	Theodore E. Deutch, FL
	Karen Bass, CA
X	William Keating, MA
X	David Cicilline, RI
X	Ami Bera, CA
	Lois Frankel, FL
	Tulsi Gabbard, HI
X	Joaquin Castro, TX
X	Robin Kelly, IL
	Brendan Boyle, PA
X	Dina Titus, NV
	Norma Torres, CA
X	Brad Schneider, IL
	Tom Suozzi, NY
	Adriano Espaillat, NY
X	Ted Lieu, CA

The List That's Freaking Out Everyone in Moscow

Congress ordered the Trump administration to submit a roster of Russians tied closely to the Kremlin. Used wisely, it can be a powerful tool.

By ANDERS ÅSLUND and DANIEL FRIED

December 18, 2017

Share on Facebook Share on Twitter

Congress hit a nerve in Moscow last summer when it passed (and President Donald Trump signed) H.R. 3364, the "Countering America's Adversaries Through Sanctions Act." Beyond the law's many sanctions, its Section 241 requires the administration to submit to Congress a detailed report identifying "the most significant senior foreign political figures and oligarchs in the Russian Federation, as determined by their closeness to the Russian regime and their net worth" within 180 days.

Judging by the decibel level in Moscow, and intense activity by Washington lobbyists on behalf of Russian clients, many in the Russian elite would hate to be fingered as being creatures of Russian President Vladimir Putin. It's clear why: Being named in this report could lead to future U.S. sanctions, and the threat of being cut off from the dollar and American banking system can be crippling; even without sanctions, being listed would make it harder to do business in the West. In their anxiety lies our opportunity, if we use it wisely.

The purpose of sanctions is to change behavior. First, the prospect of being named in the "Kremlin Report" (as we have called it) can incentivize the more independent of the Russian elite to keep some distance from Putin. Second, it can suggest to the elite that Putin's aggression — against his neighbors and the West — can have bad consequences for them personally and should be avoided. Finally, the report may subject those named to increased scrutiny by the administration for corrupt behavior such as money laundering, helping the U.S. protect the American financial system from bad actors. The Kremlin Report thus can drive a wedge between the Kremlin and some in the wider Russian elite.

How can the U.S. get this Kremlin Report right? In an Atlantic Council policy brief we wrote with our Russian colleagues Andrei Illarionov and Andrei Piontkovsky, we urged the U.S. government to apply three criteria: a person's closeness to the Russian regime, whether the person made a fortune through corrupt commercial operations with the Putin regime or whether the person held or channeled assets for the Russian leader in a seemingly corrupt fashion.

Applying these criteria, we identified seven categories of people and enterprises for inclusion in the report: (1) those responsible for aggressive, corrupt or criminal operations within or outside the Russia; (2) Putin's close circle of contemporary friends from St. Petersburg, with whom he has done business since the early 1990s, known as his "cronies"; (3) "golden children" of the rich who have become very wealthy top executives at a tender age; (4) personal friends of Putin who, to shield the president from scrutiny, hold considerable wealth for him; (5) so-called oligarchs: big businessmen profiting greatly from direct business with the Kremlin; (6) corrupt state enterprise managers who owe their positions to their close personal relations with Putin and utilize their positions for gross larceny; and; (7) the relevant companies owned by these people.

Even in a place as closed off as today's Russia, ample and reliable sources exist to identify these people. The U.S. government already started to do so in its personal sanctions against cronies since March 2014 (full disclosure: Dan Fried played a part in the design of U.S. sanctions against Russia while at the State Department). In the spring of 2016, the Panama Papers added important information, and Putin's cronies have defended themselves by transferring plenty of their wealth to family members.

The Kremlin Report should not just list Russia's wealthy in an indiscriminate fashion. Not all Russia's rich are alike. Many made their fortunes before Putin and, to survive, are forced to pay large tributes to the Kremlin. To include such people in the Kremlin Report would not appear consistent with the intent of Section 241 of the new sanctions law. On the contrary, the aim should be to provide wealthy Russian businessmen with incentives to maintain whatever independence they can from the Kremlin.

Incentives can work through differentiation. The Western sanctions on Crimea have convinced most big Russian private companies and even most large Russian state companies to avoid business there. Increased Kremlin pressure on decent private businessmen has prompted many of them to quietly sell their assets in Russia and leave the country.

Section 241 allows the U.S. government to either publicize or keep secret its choice of people and enterprises. There seems to be substantial pressure from Congress to throw together a big list. In our view, the list should be at least 40 names—but focused on the worst rather than be large. That will demonstrate its credibility, and separate the truly bad actors from the merely coerced. And it should not necessarily be the last list. We recommend keeping open the possibility of adding names to the Kremlin Report in the future. New information could come to light about bad actors missed the first time around. Keeping the list open would also extend the incentive to Russians to act with caution to avoid being named (being named on the list will not automatically mean being sanctioned, but it could be close in practice).

A well-constructed public list, naming the worst of the elite, will best serve America's interest (and arguably the free world's) in responding to past and current Russian aggression, and discouraging it in the future.

Statement for the Record
Submitted by Mr. Connolly of Virginia

The United States maintains dozens of sanctions regimes targeting countries, individuals, and behavior that threaten U.S. national security interests. Sanctions are a means to a policy outcome, and it is important to remember that this foreign policy tool, which has a mixed record at best, is not an end in itself. Sanctions also do not exist within a vacuum. U.S. credibility and the ability to drive an international consensus are key to the successful implementation of any sanctions policy. It is for these reasons that the Trump Administration's attacks on the Iranian nuclear deal, obstruction of diplomatic efforts on the Korean Peninsula, and failure to respond to Russian attacks on our free and fair elections are an existential threat to the long-term viability of sanctions as an effective U.S. foreign policy tool.

According to a 2007 analysis by the Peterson Institute for International Economics, sanctions were at least partially successful at achieving stated objectives in 34 percent of documented cases since World War I. Sanctions that sought modest policy changes were successful more than half the time, whereas sanctions aimed at regime change or military impairment had a 30 percent success ratio. Cases that achieved these latter major policy changes tended to involve strong levels of international cooperation, higher costs to the target when sanctions fail, and higher levels of trade between senders and targets than in failed cases. Studies like the Peterson analysis help to guide the application of sanctions. The Government Accountability Office has not conducted such a review of U.S. sanctions policy since 1992, and I believe it is past time for Congress to request an update to that important work.

When Iranian President Hassan Rouhani assumed office in 2013, he publicly acknowledged that sanctions were crippling Iran's economy and resolved to settle the nuclear standoff. Through a combination of concerted international diplomacy and a comprehensive global sanctions regime, the Obama Administration successfully negotiated the Joint Comprehensive Plan of Action (JCPOA), which effectively blocked Iran's path to a nuclear weapon. Throughout that process, the United States led an international coalition with the shared goal of thwarting Tehran's nuclear weapons program. The importance of international unity in this effort cannot be understated. Unilateral U.S. sanctions hold limited leverage when the United States barely registers on Iran's radar of trading partners. Several predictors of the success of a sanctions regime identified by the Peterson analysis were present in the case of the Iranian nuclear program, and the JCPOA continues to serve as a safe and viable alternative to a nuclear-armed Iran.

Despite lacking evidence of Iranian violations of the agreement, President Trump declined to certify Iran's compliance with the JCPOA last October and continues to threaten U.S. withdrawal. The United States faces a range of threats from Iran, including its ballistic missile testing, support for terrorism, destabilizing regional actions, and gross violations of human rights, further evidenced by its violent crackdown of recent domestic protests. However, none of these dangers is more perilous than the prospect of a nuclear-armed Tehran. President Trump's actions not only enable that outcome, but they also undermine the carrot and stick nature of sanctions policy and the ability of the U.S. to achieve foreign policy goals through the creation of international sanctions regimes. Who among even our allies will stand with us if we cannot live up to our commitments?

In North Korea, the U.S. has implemented strict and comprehensive international sanctions to coerce Kim Jong-Un's regime to reverse its nuclear weapons program. But why would North Korea submit to these pressures when the Trump Administration has demolished U.S. credibility to uphold international agreements that we helped to orchestrate? To reiterate, sanctions work best when there is a carrot as well as a stick. President Trump has engaged in Twitter tantrums against Kim Jong-Un, while simultaneously kneecapping his own Secretary of State's diplomatic efforts. The Korean Peninsula has been the number one global flashpoint for Trump's entire tenure, and it was not until mid-December that he finally nominated an Ambassador to South Korea and an Assistant Secretary of State for the Bureau of East Asian and Pacific Affairs. No one can observe the North Korea policy emanating from the White House and credibly say they recognize the outline of a carrot for North Korea.

When it comes to Russia, the Trump Administration cannot seem to find its sanctions pen. More than one year ago, on January 6, 2017, the U.S. Intelligence Community released an unclassified report detailing an unprecedented, deliberate, and multi-faceted campaign by Russia to interfere in the 2016 U.S. presidential election. Since then, each day there are more troubling revelations than the last that make clear senior-level Trump officials had undisclosed direct contact with Russian officials during the campaign and the transition. Special Counsel Robert Mueller has already charged four of these officials, including Trump's National Security Advisor and campaign chairman, as part of an ongoing FBI investigation into Russian election interference and the Trump Administration's murky ties to Russia.

Despite these findings, President Trump has maintained an inexplicable "bromance" with Russian President Vladimir Putin. Trump has failed to use the authorities given to him by Congress to sanction anyone involved in these attacks on American democratic institutions or take action to prevent their repetition. Last year, Ranking Member Engel and I introduced H.R. 530, the SECURE Our Democracy Act, which would publicly identify and authorize sanctions against foreign persons and governments that unlawfully interfere in U.S. federal elections. Our legislation was referred to this Committee, and we need to mark it up without delay.

In Russia, Iran, and North Korea, critical U.S. national security priorities are at risk, including the integrity of American democratic institutions and nuclear non-proliferation, particularly among our adversaries. Sanctions are a tool that could help achieve U.S. foreign policy goals in each of these countries and others, when implemented in concert with a comprehensive strategy that incorporates diplomatic efforts as well. The Trump Administration fails to grasp the broader picture, and instead seems to operate an id-driven foreign policy.

Questions for the Record from Rep. William R. Keating
To Mr. Adam Szubin and Mr. Juan Zarate
Sanctions and Financial Pressure: Major National Security Tools
January 10, 2018

Question:

Black Markets: We have moved forward with a number of sanctions regimes, however, how effective are we at addressing the black markets that emerge when the traditional channels are no longer available due to the implementing of sanctions?

Answer:

Mr. Adam Szubin's Response

Illicit actors will often react to sanctions or other pressure by trying to evade oversight, and that can certainly involve moving to the black market as a way to move money and/or goods. This is why it is so important that, in addition to targeting bad actors, we also work to strengthen international anti-money laundering and counter-terrorist financing (AML/CFT) regimes. The international financial system is only as strong as its weakest links, and we need to ensure that governments around the world are implementing the strong standards that the world has set. The last ten years have seen a lot of progress on this front, although more work is certainly needed.

Mr. Juan Zarate's Response

Mr. Zarate did not submit a response in time for printing.

Question:

Bangladesh: In light of concerning developments in the country, as well as the national security risks presented by ongoing serious rule of law issues in Bangladesh, what options should the United States be considering in terms of sanctions or other financial pressures?

- What kind of interagency cooperation is necessary to implement any of those options, and are the key actors in place in the State Department and other federal agencies to be able to effectively monitor and implement any sanctions policies, were they to be put in place?

Answer:

<u>Mr. Adam Szubin's Response</u>
Respectfully, now being out of government, I am not able to respond in an informed manner to this question. I would defer to my former colleagues at the State and Treasury Departments.

<u>Mr. Juan Zarate's Response</u>

Mr. Zarate did not submit a response in time for printing.